AF623726

OFFICE MANAGEMENT
FOR
PUBLIC ADMINISTRATION

Other Books by the Author

1. *Organisation of the State Government in Maharashtra* [Himalaya-1990]
2. *Organisation of the State Government in Maharashtra* (in Marathi) [Himalaya-1995]
3. *Electoral Reforms in India* [Wheelers Publishing - 1996].

About the Author

Dr. S.S. Gadkari is a retired Joint Secretary to the Government of Maharashtra who has also worked as Chief Administrative Officer. CIDCO, Dy. Metropolitan Commissioner, BMRDA and as Work-Study Officer in Government. At present he is working as the Executive Joint Secretary of the Maharashtra Branch of the Indian Institute of Public Administration.

He received his initial training in Work-Study from the Special Reorganisation Unit (SRU) of the Ministry of Finance in 1961 and later on from the Indian Institute of Public Administration, New Delhi. Thereafter he secured a Diploma and later on a Masters Degree in Management from the Jamnalal Bajaj Institute of the Bombay University. He was awarded a Doctorate in Public Administration in 1988.

Dr. Gadkari is keenly interested in the application of Management techniques and principles to Government work and has carried out several management studies for the Government of Maharashtra, some non-government organisations in Maharashtra and one study for the Government of India (Department of Administrative Reforms).

He has been on the guest faculty of a number of institutions in Maharashtra including, the Jamnalal Bajaj Institute of Management, the Narsee Monjee Institute of Management, the Yeshwantrao Chavan Academy, Pune, the Engineering Staff College, Nashik and the All India Institute of Local Self-Government, Bombay.

He has so far written about 40 articles and 3 books.

OFFICE MANAGEMENT
FOR
PUBLIC ADMINISTRATION
Principles and Techniques

S.S. GADKARI
Ph.D.
Executive Joint Secretary
Indian Institute of Public Administration
Maharashtra Regional Branch
Mantralaya, Bombay 400 032

CONCEPT PUBLISHING COMPANY, NEW DELHI-110059

All rights reserved. No part of this work may be reproduced, translated stored in a retrieval system, or transmitted in any form or by any means, electronic, mechanical, photocopying, recording or otherwise, without the prior written permission of the copyright owner and the publishers.

ISBN 81-7022-597-3 (HB)

ISBN 81-7022-648-1 (PB)

First Published 1997

© S.S. **Gadkari** (*b*. 1922-)

Published and Printed by
Ashok Kumar Mittal
Concept Publishing Company
A/15-16, Commercial Block, Mohan Garden
New Delhi-110059. (India)
Phones : 5504042, 5554042

TO
THE LATE PROF. N. S. PARDASANI
MY
FIRST GURU IN MANAGEMENT

— S. S. Gadkari

FOREWORD

It is more than a hundred years since Fredrick Taylor first formulated the principles of Management which have now developed into a sophisticated discipline taught at the Universities and special Institutes of Management.

Most of our Government offices and officers are, however, still not well conversant with modern principles and techniques of Management. Our offices are still run with the help of manuals prepared before the Second World War for the limited requirements of a Government concerned basically with law and order and with very limited volume of work.

Government offices have, therefore, to adopt modern principles and methods of work without forgetting that there are some fundamental differences between Government and private business and that the principles and methods used in private business are not applicable *in toto* to Government work. There are also certain principles in our old manuals which cannot be thrown overboard.

Dr. S.S. Gadkari who has the experience of Government work and the knowledge of modern Managememt, has now made a sincere and unique attempt to combine the advantages of both our traditional principles and modern techniques, in a form which can be understood even by the junior-most Government employee.

I would recommend this book to all Government Offices not only in Maharashtra but all over of the country.

General Administration Deptt.
Mantralaya, Bombay-400 032

V. S. GOPALAKRISHNAN
Additional Chief Secretary
Administrative Reforms
Govt. of Maharashtra

PREFACE

Out of my 37 years in Government service, I spent only about 7 years in the field of administrative reforms (from 1961 to 1967) as a work-study officer after some training by the Special Reorganisation Unit of the Ministry of Finance in Delhi. This was the most constructive and rewarding period of my service which led me to the regular study of Management for which fortunately the Jamnalal Bajaj Institute of the Bombay University provided facilities by way of part-time courses. Later on, I also got opportunities to teach this subject at some of the training institutes of the Government of Maharashtra and it was at the suggestion of a member of the faculty of the Yeshwantrao Chavan Academy at Pune that I have attempted this book.

Even after retirement, I continued to have deep interest in the application of management principles and techniques to Government work which, as the examples in this book would convince the reader, can be useful in Government offices.

However, most Government employees including many senior Government officers are unaware of or have serious doubts about the utility of these principles and techniques in Government work. It is my desire and hope that this book will inspire more Government employees to take interest in the subject.

It should be noted that this book deals only with *Office Management for Public Administration* and *not* with *Management in Public Administration* which is a much larger subject.

S.S. GADKARI

CONTENTS

1

WHAT IS MANAGEMENT ?

According to the Oxford dictionary, to "manage" means to handle, to conduct, to control or to take charge of something. In a way we "manage" whatever we do, whether efficiently, inefficiently or indifferently. Management is, therefore, as old as life. Even a small organism like the amoeba "manages" to survive by adapting itself to the environment. Larger organisms like a pack of wolves or lions "manage" by their combined efforts, to catch a nimble animal like a gazelle. Human beings "manage" more complicated jobs like tending large herds of animals, growing foodgrains, reaping and storing them and even selling them or operating machines.

2. With the invention of machines, large factories began to come up and managing them became a complicated job. Upto the end of the nineteenth century, they somehow managed these factories and the business arising from them, without giving much thought to the methods of management. Factory owners earned profits more by heartless exploitation of their workers than by efficient methods of managing their resources. Their attitudes (if not their instruments and methods) were not very different from those of the Egyptians in building their pyramids with the help of slave labour.

3. Towards the end of the nineteenth century, an engineer named Fredrick Taylor who worked as a supervisor in a small steel factory in America, made a systematic study of the tools and the methods used by the workers, with the help of a stopwatch and showed that the output of a worker could be increased several times by the use of proper tools and training him in scientific methods of work. He also studied the work of mangers and felt that they too needed a change in their ideas about their role and functions. He published his ideas in the form of a book titled

"The Principles of Scientific Management" which was translated into several languages. Very soon scientific management which was also referred to as "Taylorism" by the common people, was adopted by a large number of industrial establishments especially in America. Some of these methods were also tried by the armed forces of the United States of America during the First World War, and the Allied armies were amazed by the efficiency of the American army especially in the management of supplies and services.

4. About this time, some other pioneers like Gilbreth (who was only a brick-layers' supervisor) and Gantt had been making similar studies in other fields. Gilbreth in particular, studied the movements of workers at work to see how they could be minimised to reduce the strain on the worker. For example, if the tools of a worker are kept at some distance from his working table, he will have to get up or stretch his hands every time he needs a tool, which means not only waste of effort but also time. In a modern factory, one often sees a worker's tools hanging from a belt above his head and can be picked up by him even without looking at them.

5. After the end of the First World War, the principles and techniques developed by these pioneers, merged into what came to be called techniques of "Time and Motion" study which, with the addition of some more techniques later on developed into the science of "Work Study".

6. In due course, the use of these techniques was also extended to offices (even Government offices) but at that stage their application was limited to routine mechanical work in offices like, typing, stamping or filling up forms and registers.

7. About this time some academics and managers had been thinking of improvements in other aspects of work such as the structure of the organisation, communication within the organisation, or the functions of supervisors. (It is interesting to note that the principles of organisational structure were taken by these thinkers from some of the Government organisations like the army and the Roman Catholic Church (which is more like a large Government organisation spread over several countries).

8. These principles of organisation in particular, were found vary useful for offices and together with the principles of work study developed by engineers, merged into a separate branch called "Organisation and Methods" (or O & M). Some people prefer to call it "Organisation & Management".

9. In 1927, Prof. Elton Mayo in the USA carried out some very interesting experiments known as the Hawthorne Experiments on the lines of Taylor's experiments to determine the effect of physical factors like

light, temperature, rest pauses etc. on the output of workers and made the startling discovery that the output of workers was also affected to a great extent by psychological factors like the treatment given to them by their supervisors, their living conditions at home and their relationship with fellow workers. Earlier, thinkers like Mary Parker Follet or Henri Fayol had already been stressing the importance of the psychological factors in work but the Hawthorne Experiments proved it scientifically and led to the development of the Human Relations movement and later on the elaborate theories of organisation based on socio-psychological factors developed by thinkers like Simon, Bernard, Likert, Argyris, McGregor and others.

10. Simultaneously with this development in the socio-psychological fields, the mechanical aspects of management were also further refined by new techniques like value analysis, various techniques of financial management like Discounted Cash Flow (DCF) and Cost accounting. Finally came Operations Research which involves the use of very sophisticated mathematical and statistical techniques in problems of management. (It is again interesting to note that this technique of Operations Research also originated in Government during the Second World War). The development and use of these sophisticated mathematical techniques was further helped by the emergence of computers.

11. Today, therefore, the river of Management thought has two broad, streams–one is the scientific or quantitative aspect of management and the other the behavioural or socio-psychological aspect.

12. Instead of looking at different aspects of an organisation in a fragmented way as was done by the old work-study or O&M officers, the modern Management man first looks at the Organisation as a whole—as a "system" which reacts with the environment. He examines the inputs (or the expenditure) in terms of the 4'M's viz. Men, Material, Money and Minutes (*i.e.* time) and tries to compare them with the *outputs* of the system *i.e.,* what the system produces. The ratio of the outputs to inputs is called productivity. In mathematical terms....

$$\text{Productivity} = \frac{\text{Output}}{\text{Input}}$$

13. This measure of productivity can be applied to compare the productivity of two similar machines or the productivity of two workers working with the same machine but when you try to compare the productivity of two machines or two organisations producing different

types of goods it can only be in terms of the most common measure of inputs and outputs which is money. It is necessary to know the value of all the inputs and outputs *in terms of money* to compare the productivity of two dissimilar organisations or two machines producing different types of goods.

14. If you are not satisfied with the productivity of an organisation (or system), you have to examine the working of different parts of the system (called sub-systems) and for this the original techniques of work study, value analysis etc. are still very useful.

15. A question is often asked whether Management is a science or an art. The practical answer is that it is both an art and a science. The mechanical and mathematical stream of management is more like a science while the use of socio-psychological factors is more like an art.

2

MANAGEMENT AND GOVERNMENT

To what extent are the principles and techniques of Management applicable to Government organisations? (Throughout this book, when we refer to Government organisations, they include quasi-Governmental organisations like municipalities or Zilla Parishads or even some social-service organisations (often referred to as N.G.Os.) whose primary function is some service without profit.

2. Many senior administrators are often inclined to pooh-pooh Management as something not applicable to Government. When the Fulton Committee in the U.K. recommended the re-orientation of the British Civil Service towards Management, a senior administrator said that "a Secretary to Government was a different kind of animal from the manager of a company". On the other hand, many people especially from the private sector see in Management the cure for all the ills of Government. Immediately after Independence a number of Governments all over the country engaged private Management consultants to suggest improvements in Government methods of work. Most of these efforts proved disappointing. This is somewhat surprising considering that some of the most important principles of Management and even sophisticated techniques like Operations Research originated in Government. To understand this paradox let us first understand some of the basic differences between Government and the private sector.

(i) The first characteristic of Government is the vast range of its functions which include defence, communication, social services like education or health, provision of some essential goods like water or electricity or public transport and even some economic goods like industrial plots or fertilisers or seeds. While some of the goods or services can be priced like commercial goods, most of the services and even some of the commercial goods and services are supplied by Government either free or at heavily subsidised rates, often as a monopoly.

(ii) Second, many of these functions of Government conflict with each other. An increase in educational facilities can lead to an increased demand for jobs for the educated (which are more costly to create) and lead to increased unemployment of the educated. An irrigation project can improve the economic condition of families below the dam but creates problems of displacement for many families above the dam. Large- scale industrialisation can create employment and wealth but also gives rise to problems of environment. This conflict makes decision making a difficult and slow process in Government. Decisions are often compromises and therefore economically less efficient.

(iii) The Private Sector produces mostly goods and commercial services for profit. On the other hand, Government provides mostly services not for profit but for the benefit of the people. Even if a Government commercial organisation like one manufacturing pharmaceuticals or fertilisers makes a large profit, there will be a demand for the reduction of the prices of its products. (At present most of them are run at a loss). Even if a department of Government not engaged in any commercial activities (like the Department of Education or Public Health) shows a large saving in the grant allotted to it, the Public Accounts Committee will ask for an explanation why it overestimated its requirement of funds.

(iv) A private commercial company can subsist and maintain itself only on its profits. If the company fails to make any profits continuously for a few years, it will have to close down. On the other hand Government is sustained essentially by funds provided by the people through taxes, fees, loans (including subscription to schemes like the National Savings Certificates or Public Provident Funds which are also loans to Government).

(v) The other source for the sustenance of Government is *authority* given by laws to tax people, to arrest and punish people, to make them work compulsorily for Government (for example as conscripts in a war) and to place their properties at the disposal of Government whenever required as at the time of war or an election or when it acquires land for a public work). Even a large private sector company has no authority to tax people or to take over their properties without the consent of the owners.

The levy of taxes, the collection of money through Provident Funds or National Saving Certificates, the requisitioning or acquisition of property is all done through laws and rules made or approved by the Legislature which represents the people. In granting this authority to Government, the Legislature is also keen to see that this authority is not abused by Government, that the taxes levied or the properties acquired by Government are not beyond its legitimate requirements. Alleged or suspected misuse of these powers and resources can lead to a huge uproar not only in the Legislature but also in the public and in the press (which serves as the watch dog of the people). This is the principle of *accountability* of the Government to the Legislature and the people (including the press.)

There are also agencies like the courts, the Vigilance Commissions, the Lok Ayuktas to entertain complaints against arbitrary or illegal actions of Government. These agencies other than the courts, are also known by different names in different countries—Ombudsman in Scandinavian countries, Parliamentary Commissioner in England and most of the British Dominions, and Mediateur in France.

A Government officer has, therefore, to be far more careful and watchful in his actions and see that he does not over-step the powers given or the limits laid down by the laws, rules and regulations. A salesman of a private company, can on the spot agree to some reduction in price to bag a large order. A salesman of a Government company doing that will end up with a departmental enquiry. Hence the large number of rules, regulations, registers or forms in Government though , it must be admitted that all these rules and regulations are not necessarily justified by the requirements of accountability, but are often made unnecessarily rigid by over-caution, the lack of imagination, timidity, stupidity and even cupidity of Government servants.

(vi) We have defined productivity as the ratio of

$$\frac{\text{Output}}{\text{Input}}$$

In the private sector both the output as well as the input are evaluated to the last paisa or cent and it is possible to calculate and compare the poductivity of two organisations producing absolutely dissimilar products like for example motor cars and textiles.

In Government, on the other hand, the outputs which consist mostly of free or subsidised public services and amenities like security, roads, bridges, free education or free medical treatment, cannot be easily evaluated in terms of money. Even the inputs in Government are not usually costed very rigorously. For example, the rents of Government buildings, electricity charges, sweeper services are usually paid for by a department like the P.W.D. Stationery is usually supplied free to Government Departments. These are called the hidden costs in Government. If an honest effort is made, it may be possible to evaluate some of these inputs, but it is much more difficult to evaluate outputs accurately.

In general, therefore, it is difficult to evaluate the productivity of a government function or department. (In the USA they have tried to work out some special measures of productivity of Government organisations especially for the state and local Governments but most of these organisations found it rather a costly and difficult exercise.)

3. Inspite of these differences, it is possible to make use of the principles and techniques developed by industry and business, in Government work with some modifications. Quite often the more sophisticated techniques used in industry and business have to be simplified before being applied to Government work. For example, in the control of small projects, it is much better to use a simple technique like bar-charts than a more complicated one called PERT/CPM. This is something like intermediate technology used by poorer and less developed countries. Throughout this book we shall keep this approach.

3

ROLE AND FUNCTIONS OF OFFICE
Importance of Memory

An office is an essential part of any Government activity. A private medical practitioner or a petty contractor doing small jobs, does not need an office, but a Government doctor or a Government engineer doing even petty repairs, always has a small office where he keeps his papers, registers, stocks etc.

2. Government offices do a variety of jobs-such as personnel (or establishment) work, receiving and paying money and keeping accounts, construction, inspection and supervision, planning, budgeting, giving information to the public and correspondence with other offices and the public (which is usually called administrative work).

3. A large proportion of Government offices do such administrative work which usually arises from communications (letters or applications) received from outside. The action taken on such a communication in a large office is usually on the lines indicated in Annexure 3-A to this chapter. With some small variations, this is the general procedure not only for administrative work but even other types of work. (In very small field offices there is sometimes no noting on cases or no section registers.)

4. If you study the italicized words, in this procedure in the Annexure, you will notice that there are about 28 operations which include:-

I.	Recording	12 – for registration in various registers, or giving the communication some numbers (1,2,3,5,6,8,12, 21, 23, 26, 27, 28).

II.	Scrutiny of case	1 – writing a note on the communication, or scrutiny (No.9).
III.	Decision	1 – decision by the officer (No.14).
IV.	Communicating the decision	2 – drafting a reply or order (No. 10 and 17). 2 – approval of the reply by the officer (No. 15 and 19). 1 – despatching the reply (No. 24).
V.	Movement of papers	9 – times (4, 7, 11, 13, 16, 18, 20, 22, 24, 25).

5. This analysis shows that leaving aside movement of papers, there are 4 basic functions of an office viz:-

(1) Keeping *Record* (or Memory) (12 Steps)
(2) Noting or *Scrutiny* of the case (1 step)
(3) Taking a *Decision*; (1 step)
(4) *Communicating* the decision (5 steps).

6 . Out of these, the first one viz. Record is to keep track of the case to enable the office to locate it whenever it is required later. This is also called the "Memory" function of office because the record serves as the "Memory" of the office which has to be recalled from time to time. Even laws, rules or Government orders which form part of the record, are a kind of crystallised memory of the office because they are based on some past experience either in one's own office or elsewhere.

7. To an outsider it may appear that too much time and effort is spent on keeping a record of a case and its movement. Though it may be possible to reduce some of this recording, it cannot be eliminated altogether. It is necessitated by the severe accountability of Government explained in the previous Chapter. In a private company, the misplacement of a letter can lead to some monetary loss and possibly even the dismissal of some employee; but in the case of Government, it can lead not only to loss but a furore in the Legislature and the Press and sometimes even a crisis for Government. Therefore, one cannot eliminate all these registers and records in Government, though one can certainly reduce some of the registers depending upon the nature of the work and the size of the offices. This problem has been considered in Chapter 10 to 13 on Work-simplification.

In the experiment with the Desk Officer system in Maharashtra, (see Chap. 9), some of these registers (including work-sheets of Assistants) were eliminated. This led to chaos in most of the departments and ultimately they had to be restored.

8. The reader should note the manner in which the procedure has been recorded in Annexure 3 A. It is very useful for analysing and simplifying procedures and reducing delays (See Chapters 10-13)

9. Of the four functions viz. Memory, Scrutiny, Decision and Communication, the Memory function is the basic function of an office because the other functions depend upon the record or the Memory of the office. The importance of decisions depends upon the level of the office and the nature of the problem— whether it is a routine situation or an extra-ordinary situation. Even communication depends upon Memory because in giving a reply, one must take into account the replies given to the party in the past.

10. The importance of the Memory of office can be appreciated from a unique experience of the present author in a public undertaking. In 1973, a high level Mission of the World Bank visited a State Secretariat for preliminary scouting for projects. All the Departments were asked to prepare brief outlines (just one or two pages) of projects which could be considered for World Bank assistance. We prepared a very impressive booklet of about twenty projects, beautifully typed on an electronic typewriter and bound together with spiral binding. We received compliments from the Chief Secretary for the impressive booklet. However, the Mission just dismissed all the projects saying "This is a very impressive sheaf of projects but on going through it, we feel that no one in this organisation or in Government seems to have read the report of an earlier Mission of the World Bank which visited India about 3 years ago."

11. Next day a search started for the report of the earlier Mission. No one seemed to have heared about it. Ultimately the Personal Assistant of the concerned Secretary said that this report had been received about three years ago and had been kept in a cupboard in the then Secretary's room. When the report was taken out, it was found that this Secretary had just picked up one small paragraph from the Report suggesting the preparation or a capital budget for the region, sent it to one organisation and kept the Report in his own personal cupboard without even informing the Deputy Secretary who had been working in the Department for more than 30 years. All the good project profiles prepared by the organisation were wasted because of the failure of the Memory function.

Ahmednagar or Lakhina Experiment

12. In the early eighties, administration in India was shaken up by what was then called the Ahmednagar or Lakhina experiment in which a young Collector named Lakhina brought about some spectacular improvement in the Collectorate of Ahmednagar. Newspapers published rave reviews about it on the front page. Teams of officers, not only from other states, but even from some of the neighbouring countries like Sri Lanka and Bangladesh visited Ahmednagar. Mr. Lakhina was also awarded "Padmashri" by the President. A major portion of the improvement made by Mr. Lakhina was about records, and the environment of the office and its surroundings. The "experiment" has been described in more detail in Appendix A.

Neglect of Records

13. Unfortunately maintenance of records in Government offices has been very badly neglected in post-Independence India. Offices always ask for more operating sections and more officers at higher level whenever a new activity crops up or there is a significant increase in the general volume of work; but rarely do they care to ask for staff for the Records Section (usually called the Registry). The people working in the Registry are also not anxious to continue in the section very long and are looking for transfers from the section. The Head of the section (usually a senior clerk) is often a person not considered fit for any other work in the office. The following suggestions are worth consideration:—

(i) There should be a person of the status of at least a Section Officer in charge of the Registry. He should have some training in the maintenance of records. He should have authority to inspect the records of all the sections.

(ii) There should be a few promotion posts for the clerks in the section; and

(iii) There should be some posts of "daftaries" (an intermediate post between a clerk and a peon) which can be given to some bright peons who have *studied upto pre-S.S.C. standard.* This will reduce the number of clerks (who are not anxious to stay in the section) and give some incentives and avenues for promotion for good peons. Essentially records work is routine and mechanical work.

Centralised vs Decentralised Records

14. A basic question about records management is whether it should be centralised or decentralised. A centralised Record section has three advantages:

(i) It can be managed with a smaller staff trained and specialised in records management;
(ii) It can bring some uniformity in the management of records in the whole office; and
(iii) It can be mechanised and even computerised.

15. Before Independence, many Government organisations (including the Bombay Secretariat) used to have centralised Records sections. As the volume of work increased, it was found difficult to manage records from a centralised section. With the rapid expansion of offices, it was also difficult to retain experienced staff in the central Records Section and so ultimately most of the record work was decentralised and transferred to the operating sections. The only work which remained with the central Registry was "Inward" registration and despatch. However, even if records work is decentralised and transferred to sections, the residuary Registry should have some power of supervision over records in all Sections.

Computerisation

16. It is also possible to computerise some of the records work— particularly the numerous registers in which the movement of files are recorded. This question has been discussed in Chapter 15 on office-machines.

Role of Office

17. Finally, one must realise that however high-placed one may be, the real work of Government is being done by the people in the field— by engineers, doctors, teachers, police officers and even Collectors and Tehsildars. The role of the offices especially those at higher levels is essentially to carry out the administrative tasks. Office workers should try to understand the problems of these field workers and help them to solve these problems instead of creating more problems for them. This is a point which many office workers forget.

ANNEXURE 3-A

PROCESSING OF A LETTER IN A LARGE OFFICE

Registry Clerk	(1) *Stamps* the letter
	(2) *Enters* it in the general Inward Register.
	(3) *Enters* the number in the Inward Register on the letter.
	(4) *Sends* to Section concerned.
Section Clerk	(5) Enters it in the Section Registers.
	(6) Gives it an Index or subject *classification number*.
	(7) *Gives* it to dealing assistant.
Dealing Assistant	(8) *Enters* it in his *worksheet.*
	(9) *Writes* a note.
	(10) *Drafts* a reply.
	(11) *Gives* to Section clerk.
Section Clerk	(12) *Takes entry* in Section Register.
	(13) *Sends* to officer.
Officer	(14) *Passes* orders.
	(15) *Approves* draft *reply.*
	(16) *Returns* to section.
Dealing Assistant	(17) *Prepares fair copy* of the draft reply.
	(!8) *Submits* to Officer.
Officer	(19) *Signs* the fair copies.
	(20) *Returns* to office.
Section Clerk	(21) *Takes note* in the Section Register.
	(22) *Sends* fair copies to the Despatch Section.
Despatch Clerk	(23) *Takes note* in Despatch Register.
	(24) *Despatches* letter.
	(25) *Returns* office copy to Section.
Dealing Assistant	(26) *Gives order* to record papers or keep in await.
Section Clerk	(27) *Takes note* in Section Register
	(28) *Files* papers or keeps in await.

4

RECORDS MANAGEMENT (1)
Preservation

As explained in the last chapter, records or Memory is by far the most important function of an office and all other functions including decisions and even communication of decisions depend upon records.

2. A Government office can be recognised from a distance from the large stacks of brown-yellow dust-covered papers reaching upto the ceiling. Despite this ocean of papers (or probably because of it), Government offices can rarely locate a paper quickly. Cases are delayed for weeks -sometimes even months, for want of papers. Reminders are usually useless. If you go down to the office, the first reply you receive is that your letter or previous papers are not traceable. All this is because of poor management of records. (Whenever one goes to a Government Office to enquire about any communication—even in an official capacity—it is advisable to carry a copy of the original letter, and hand it over to the person who tells you that your letter is not traceable).

3. Records Management has two aspects viz. :

(i) Preservation and storage of records ; and
(ii) Retrieval of records.

Preservation and Storage of Papers

4. The papers in a Government office can be divided into two main categories —(I) Live papers *i.e.,* papers on which action has not been completed : and (II) Closed papers *i.e.,* those on which action has been completed.

(I) Live Papers include

(1) ***Current Papers*** : *i.e.* Papers on which action is still to be taken or is being taken.

(2) ***Await Papers*** : Which have been examined and on which some preliminary action may even have been taken but on which further action is held up for information or decision from some other offices or courts.

(3) ***Periodical returns*** :

(a) Which are required to be submitted by the office to superior offices,

(b) Which are received by the office from other offices; and

(c) Registers in which this information is sometimes entered.

(II) Closed papers

These are usually divided into 4 classes A, B, C and D as explained below :

A. Class : Records required to be preserved more or less permanently. These include files of historical importance , long term agreements especially about lands, town-planning and similar maps, plans of important Government buildings, important policy orders, important court cases, papers about legislation...etc.

B. Class : Records which are required to be maintained for 30-40 years. An important part of this record, are papers relating to employees who usually serve for about 30-35 years. (Formerly these records were usually required to be kept for 30 years but in view of the increased age of retirement and the fact that at present most employees join Government service at a fairly early age, this period should now be increased to 40 years.

C. Class : Records which are likely to be required for a short period of 5-10 years such as papers about various applications to Government, yearly distribution of grants, budgets etc. In some states, this record is further divided into two classes —

C_1, Class — preserved for 15 years.
C_2, Class — preserved for 5 years.

D. Class: Correspondence of absolutely transient importance which need not be preserved for more than one year. This includes requests for some petty information or forms, copies of orders issued by other offices which are not of much concern to this office.

Each Department/Office has to draw up a list of subjects the files on which are required to be preserved according to the A/B/C/D classification given above.

Storage of Record

5. Live papers in the above list as well as closed records of D class, should be kept by the dealing Assistant. D Class record should be destroyed after a year.

Closed record of C class should be kept in the operating sections but not necessarily by the dealing Assistant.

In many offices there are special clerks or daftaries in charge of such papers.

A and B class closed record should be kept in a separate Record room in the office, if available.

6. In many Revenue Department offices of Maharashtra, A and B class records are kept in a common Record room of the office but tied in cloth in different colors with the file numbers and year written in black ink on the cloth. The cloth protects the records from dust.

7. There cannot be any hard and fast rules about storage which will differ from office to office depending upon the volume and the importance of the record in each category and the available space. One should however, judge the importance of the space factor from some interesting statistics given by Mr. N. Rangarajan Director of the Institute of Secretariat Training and Management, in his "Monograph on Records Management" (1974) :

(i) Ministries/Departments of the Government of India created (in 1974) annually about 5.75 lakh files;

(ii) The National Archives of India which at that time kept files upto the year 1947, had shelves measuring 14-15 miles in length;

(iii) If all the Ministries (excluding subordinate and field offices), were to transfer to the National Archives, all the post-1947 records, it would require 110 miles of shelves-or about 8 more National Archives; and

(iv) The annual build-up of files of all the administrative offices of the Govt. of India excluding field agencies like the Railways and the Post and Telegraph Department, was estimated to require 8 miles of shelves every year (in 1974).

Cost of Storage

8. One must 'therefore' take into account the cost of storage of records.

Mr. Rangarajan had estimated in 1974 that the cost of storage per section in an area like the Parliament Street in Delhi was nearly Rs. 2800, per month per section.

9. I would suggest a slightly different yardstick. An open rack or closed almirah occupies nearly 10 sq. ft. of space (allowing about 2 ft. in front for the clerks or peons). The cost of space at the Nariman Point in Bombay is at least Rs. 10,000 per sq. ft. or Rs. 1,00,000 per rack. (In Bombay and many large cities no accommodation is available on rental basis). The number of files on a rack can vary depending upon the method of filing and the size of the file. Assuming an average of about 200 files per rack, the cost of space would be about Rs. 500 per file in Bombay. Even in a medium size city where the cost of built up space would be about Rs. 500-600, per sq. ft. the capital cost of storage would be about Rs. 20-25 per file.

10. These figures are not meant to be standard yardsticks for calculating costs but only to give an idea of the importance of minimising the stored records by weeding out periodically the useless papers.

Need for Weeding Records

11. In pre-Independence days, even with very limited work, there used to be in the Bombay Secretariat, two or three clerks permanently weeding out records— *i.e.*

(a) destroying records which had outlived their utility according to the A,B, C, D classification explained above; and
(b) removing from the records to be retained, unimportant papers like reminders, duplicate copies, interim notes and replies etc.

12. Today despite the huge increase in the volume of work and record, there is no systematic weeding out of records. In the Ahmednagar experiment referred to earlier, the Collector got rid of 20 truckloads of paper and realised nearly Rs. 25,000 by the sale of this old record which had not been weeded out for several years.

Lamination

13. Papers like agreements, maps, drawings etc. which are required to be preserved permanently or for long periods, should be laminated. Lamination is a process by which the paper gets coated with a thin layer of plastic. Laminating machines should be installed at the headquarters of each district preferably in an office like the Land Records Department which would need it the most.

5

RECORDS MANAGEMENT (2)
Classification and Retrieval

1. Record or memory, however, well preserved, is useless, unless it can be retrieved or recalled quickly. The first requirement of a Retrieval system is a good system of classification or an indexing system. When the work of Government offices was very limited in volume, a simple Retrieval system which used only the Inward registration number was good enough. As the volume of work began to increase, this system proved inadequate and more elaborate indexing or classification systems began to emerge.

2. A description of indexing systems used in some of the Secretariats in India is given in Appendix-B. This Appendix has been prepared from the information supplied by the respective Governments. It is only meant to give some idea of the different types of systems in use. The following points should, however, be borne in mind.

(i) If an office has already in use an old system, which is working satisfactorily, it is not advisable to change over to a new system, unless the old system is giving serious trouble. The dislocation caused by the change is sometimes more harmful than the improvements expected from the new system.

(ii) Very sophisticated and perfectly scientific systems may not be suitable for Government offices. In 1950, a firm of private consultants in Bombay suggested for the Secretariat, the adoption of a "Decimal" system like the Dewey system used in all libraries. A committee of senior Secretaries rightly. rejected the suggestion because they felt that the Dewey system is used by librarians who have received systematic training about the system for one or two years. In Government offices the work of indexing files is usually done by the lowest level of clerks who are liable to change very frequently. The Secretaries, therefore, adopted a very practical system described in Appendix-B.

(iii) The development of a new system or its working should not be left to the clerks in the Section or even to Section Officers who have often no time and much less any aptitude for such type of work. There should, therefore, be an officer, of the rank of at least a Section Officer as head of the Record Section properly trained and supervising the indexing work in all the Sections of office.

(iv) As far as possible, do not use purely numerical systems because by itself a number does not convey any idea of the subject unless one refers to the indexing catalogue. On the other hand, in a system like that in Maharashtra or in Orissa or Punjab, (see Appendix-B), the letters in the file number immediately indicate the broad subject. For example—

BUD – for Budget
EST – for Establishment
ZPP – for Zilla Parishad

The number which follows the letters gives the detailed subject.

EST 10 – Proposals for additional staff.
EST 11 – New Recruitment
EST 12 – Promotions
EST 13 – Fixation of pay
EST 14 – Crossing efficiency bar

Under this system, even a new recruit can guess the section to which the letter pertains.

(v) Every section must have a complete list of its index numbers and no new numbers should be opened without the permission of the trained expert referred to in (iii) above.

Select Files/Guard Files etc.

3. However, perfect the office record, one cannot always refer to the original files for orders or precedents. For example, if you are dealing with a problem about taxation of properties of Embassies or Consulates there may be dozens of orders issued by the Government of India or by the respective State Government over the last fifty years. One cannot go through all the files for fifty years. For this purpose the section or the

occupant of the concerned table should keep a file containing all the important orders on the subject. Such files are called Standing Order files or Select files, or Guard files or Hand files. (There may be other names). I shall call them "select files."

4. Such files should also include, besides the orders, minutes of important decisions on the subject, any important legal opinions on the subject, statistics and important notes if any. (Such notes are often required to be prepared when a new officer takes over. If a copy of the note prepared last time is kept in the select file, it is easy to up-date it and prepare a new note. Such notes are also useful for new recruits).

5. The number of such files will depend upon the volume of orders. For example in the case of Diplomatic offices, if there are too many orders, one can prepare separate files for office-properties, residential properties, cars etc.

6. Some practical hints for the maintenance of these select files would be useful—

(a) Ring files which can be opened at any page are very convenient. One can replace any order or add a new order at any place in the file. (In the ordinary office file, one has to remove all the pages either before or after the concerned order before it can be replaced by a new one.)

(b) Select files should be supplemented by a folder containing loose copies of some of the important orders which are required to be put up with cases frequently.
In no case should the Select file be submitted with any case because it is the quintessence of the office memory on the subject. If it is lost, the whole memory of last several years may be lost.

(c) Mr. Rangarajan erstwhile Director of the Institute of Secretariat Training and Management has suggested the maintenance of —

(i) Select files
(ii) Standing Notes
(iii) Precedent Book
(iv) Reference Folder
(v) Induction Note – (for a new comer to the table)
(vi) Alphabetical list of important files; and
(vii) A printed index of the records of the Ministry.

With the present state of records and staff in most Government offices, this is rather a difficult proposition and I feel that if a Section or Assistant can maintain just a Select file on each subject and a folder with spare copies that should be enough. The standing notes, precedents etc. can all be included in the Select file.

Note Book with Alphabetical Index

7. Officers above the level of Section Officers who are in charge of two or three sections or the whole office, cannot possibly keep select files of their own on all the subjects dealt with by them and have, therefore, to depend upon whatever orders are put up by their office. Such abject dependence on office is undesirable, (even dangerous) and so officers should keep a note book or file with alphabetically indexed pages in which they should take short notes of orders, decisions etc. which come to their notice from time to time, on the following lines—

Consular Officers

(1) Cars to be given special numbers
(GR, MEA No. ....dated ....)
(2) Cars to be exempted from Vehicle Tax
(GR, MEA No. ....dated ....)
(3) Properties to be exempted from General Property tax but not from service taxes
(G.R. U.D. Deptt- No..........dated ....)

Job Description Files

8. For every table in the office there should be a Job description file which should state —

(i) the subjects allotted to the table;
(ii) the Acts, rules, regulations etc. required for each subject (with copies);
(iii) a brief description of diffrent types of cases under each subject and how to deal with them. Mention the relevant orders (which should be in the Select file);
(iv) the periodical reports or returns required to be submitted from or received by the table;
(v) Names and addresses of important offices with whom correspondence is usually required to be carried on;
(vi) any other important matters;

Such files are very useful for a new Assistant appointed to the table or even for other members of the Section if they have to deal with cases from the table in an emergency.

6

NOTING

Noting is a peculiar feature of work in Government offices. In a private business or commercial office, when a communication is received, the officer takes a decision and either dictates a letter or gives instructions to the concerned assistant. Notes are recorded only on very important cases which may have to be discussed in meetings at higher level.

2. In Government on the other hand, an assistant has to write notes on most cases, submit them to his officer who in turn may have to submit them to two or three officers above him and get a decision.

3. This system of noting and decision - making is necessitated by four factors:

(i) The severe accountability of Government to the people, the legislature and the press which keep a close watch on whatever Government does. A small mistake can bring the whole Government into disrepute.

(ii) As explained in Chapter 2, this severe accountability leads to the Government machinery being bound by laws, rules, regulations and precedents which form the Memory of the office. The repository of this Memory is the office while decisions are taken by officers who are liable to transfers. So a note is necessary to explain the case to the officer. (As explained in Chapter 9, officer oriented systems have not been very successful in Government.

(iii) No legal draftsman has so far been able to draft a perfect law or set of rules which can cover every situation. So there are always cases which cannot be covered by existing rules and such cases require to be discussed and have to be treated as exceptions or may necessitate amendment of the rules.

(iv) There are also ambiguous cases which may fall under Rule A or Rule B and the implications of the two alternatives may be widely different.

4. However, this practice of noting is sometimes carried to ridiculous length as can be seen from the following two examples from the personal experience of the present writer.

(a) The West Bengal Government once asked the Government of Bombay about the provisions in the Bombay Rent Act about eviction of tenants. An Assistant in the Bombay Secretariat put up a simple draft letter forwarding a copy of the Bombay Rent Act and inviting attention to the relevant sections of the Act. An old-fashioned Assistant Secretary reprimanded the Assistant for putting up a draft letter without a note and made him write a short note repeating whatever had been said in the draft letter.

(b) The employees of a large Public Sector Undertaking once approached the Managing Director (a Government officer of the rank of a Chief Engineer) and requested him to preside over the annual function of the employees' sports club. He asked them a number of questions about the activities of the club, its sources of finance etc. but finally asked the employees to give him a *note* incorporating all this information which they had given him orally.

5. Leaving aside such ridiculous cases, noting is essential in a large number of cases because of the reasons stated in para 3 above and it is necessary to understand how a good note should be written. Many office-workers just repeat the contents of the communication being noted upon without examining the issues involved. Such notes are only exercises in paraphrasing or conversion from "direct into indirect speech"— two favourite exercises in the teaching of English. Such notes are worse than useless because they not only do not contribute to the understanding or scrutiny of the case, but only cause wastage of time of everybody including the officer, the typist and the noting assistant himself.

6. A good note should have 5 parts—.

I. A brief statement of the proposal or problem;
II. The scrutiny which should state the Government policies, rules etc. in favour or against the proposal;
III. The alternatives before the office—(a) to accept the proposal; (b) to reject it; (c) to accept it subject to some modifications; or (d) to post-pone it;
IV. Tentative conclusion; and
V. Other departments if any, which may have to be consulted.

7. To facilitate the understanding of the case, it is advisable to itemise the issues as well as conclusions as shown in para 5 of the *specimen note* in the Annexure to this chapter. It is also convenient for reference if the paragraphs of notes are numbered.

Forms to Replace Notes

8. In many routine cases like sanctioning leave or Provident Fund loans, a note can be replaced by forms which make it easier for the officers to understand the case and take a decision. Two specimen forms have been shown in Chapter 14.

Alternative Methods of Arranging Papers

9. There are two methods of arranging papers in a file—

(i) Mixed filing in which each communication is followed by its note;
(ii) Separation of communications and notes into two sections viz:—(i) correspondence; and (ii) notes.

The first system automatically connects every note to the communication which precedes it but an officer dealing with the file has unnecessarily to go through every communication and note–many of which are just off-shoot issues or reminders which are not essential to the understanding of the main problem on the file.

10. The second system is very often preferred by officers especially at higher level who can quickly go through some important letters

and notes and size up the problem. However, it requires some time and some special effort to connect a communication to the note in the noting section.

11. The first system was being followed by most Government offices before Independence. At present many Government offices have switched over to the second system. Each system has its advantages and disadvantages.

Noting as a Source of Delays

12. Noting which is meant to help an office in decision making, especially in complicated cases, can also be a hindrance to decision-making. If there is no noting, the office or officer has got to take a decision and communicate it immediately by a letter as in private sector offices. Noting, however, gives him the lattitude to go on writing and raising issues—often irrelevant ones—and prolong a decision. (Some officers are inclined to show off their literary talents).

13. One must also mention in this connection, the habit of Government officers of raising queries or returning cases to office with instructions "to discuss" or "to bring up" the case. In 50 per cent of the cases there is nothing to discuss but it is only the inability of an officer to take a decision. Sometimes an officer who has wasted his whole day in entertaining visitors or friends, sees the mountain of files on his table in the evening and returns to office all these pending cases with instructions to "please speak" or "please discuss" or "please bring up" just to remove the cases from his table and go home leaving behind a "clean table".

14. When a case is returned with instructions like "please discuss", the Assistant has not only to spend time in discussion but has to waste considerable time in going up to the officer's cabin three or four times before he finds the officer free. The following measures are worth a trial—

(i) Prohibit the use of this practice of writing "please speak", "please discuss" and "please bring up" on cases, except for the Head of the office.

(ii) If an officer does not agree with what the office has proposed, he should either give clear cut orders or instructions about the deficiencies in the office disposal or ask for the additional information he needs or write a note himself.

(iii) An exception can be made in the case of very senior officers like the Heads of large offices who may not have the time to write out notes on all cases. Quite often they read these cases at home or on tour. Such officers may be *specifically permitted* to return the cases to office with instructions to discuss but must reserve everyday or every week a specified hour for discussion. Any member of the staff who has cases to discuss should inform the P.A. of the officer who should call these lower officers or staff one after another. This experiment was successfully tried in one office where the Head of the office was a very busy person.

These simple measures can go a long way in reducing delays in decision and the time which the staff has to waste in trying to meet the officer.

Single File System

15. Similar delays take place under the system of what is called the "Single File" system or "unofficial references". Under this system, an office or department seeking the advice or consent (called concurrence) of another department, instead of writing a letter to that department sends its own file with notes to the other department; and the latter department records its views in the form of a note below the note of the first department. The system is followed for consulation among Secretariat departments but sometimes even between a Secretariat department and its immediate subordinate offices.

16. When there is no agreement between the two departments, the file moves to and fro between the two departments with notes and counter-notes by the two departments. This noting and counter-noting sometimes goes on for months before a decision is taken.

17. Like the system of personal discussion in an office, the Single File system is meant to reduce formal correspondence and paper work but often leads to more delays and paper work. One very common point of dispute or disagreement is about which department should deal with a case, which often go on for months.

ANNEXURE 6-A

SPECIMEN NOTE

Public Health Department

The Director of Public Health has submitted a proposal to set up a Rural Hospital at Timtimpur the headquarters of Timtimpur Tehsil in Dimdimgad District. A local philanthrophist has promised to donate Rs. 75 lakhs towards the cost of the building and Rs. 15 lakhs towards equipment provided the hospital is named after his mother.

2. The Government policy is to set up one Rural Hospital in each Tehsil of the State. The standard cost of a Rural Hospital as approved by Government, is—

(i)	Building	...... Rs. 75 lakhs
(ii)	Equipment, furniture, ambulance etc.	...... Rs. 20 lakhs
(iii)	Recurring cost-salaries, supplies etc.	...... Rs. 20 lakhs p.a.

3. The donor has agreed to contribute only the cost of the building and Rs. 15 lakhs for equipment. Government will, therefore, have to bear about Rs. 5 lakhs towards equipment and the recurring cost of Rs. 20 lakhs on account of salaries etc. The Director states that the balance of the cost of equipment and the recurring cost on account of staff and equipment can be met from the normal budget provision.

4. In the Finance Department circular No. DNS 13.74 dated 14th April 1974. Government has issued instructions that Government Departments should not accept any donations which would saddle Government with recurring costs. However, this condition would not be relevant in this case because, whenever Government sets up a rural hospital in this Tehsil (according to its policy) it would have to bear the recurring cost (in addition to the capital and non-recurring cost which the donor has agreed to bear almost wholly). There is also no objection to naming the hospital after the donor's mother. The Finance Department may, therefore, agree to the proposal.

5. However, there is one snag in respect of the proposal. As against the Government objective of establishing one Rural Hospital per Tehsil, so far hospitals have been established in 112 out of 210 Tehsils of 20 districts or approximately 53 per cent of the Tehsils. This distribution is however, not uniform and the proportion varies from 3 out of 10 Tehsils (30%) in Thanthanpur District to 8 out of 11 Tehsils (72%) in Dimdimgad District and 8 out of 10 Tehsils (80%) in Abadi-Abad District. The proportion of Rural Hospitals in Dimdimgad District is already one of the highest in the state and there can be complaints from other districts of the State. However, even if we reject the proposal on this ground, the saving of Rs. 20-25 lakhs will not be sufficient for an additional hospital in any other district. Further, Government will lose a hefty contribution of nearly Rs. 75 lakhs. The case for a hospital at Timtimpur can be stronger if the donor agrees to contribute an additional Rs. 5 lakhs towards equipment so that Government will not have to bear any part of the cost of equipment.

6. To summarise:

(i) The donor may be asked to donate an additional amount of Rs. 5 lakhs towards equipment;
(ii) Irrespective of whether the donor accepts the proposal or not, Government may agree to accept the proposal and build a Rural Hospital at Timtimpur; and
(iii) Government may agree to bear the whole of the recurring cost on account of the hospital.

7. Before action is taken on these lines, the file may be shown to–

(a) the Finance Department with reference to para 4 above;
(b) the Planning Department with reference to para 5 above.

Section Officer

Under Secretary.

Dy. Secretary.

7

COMMUNICATION (1) : Types

The end product of most administrative work is a written communication. As far as possible, oral communications should be avoided except in an emergency. Even in such cases, the oral communication should be followed by a written communication. One comes across many cases in which government officers acting on the basis of an oral order had to repent because the person who gave the oral instructions later on denied having issued them.

2. If one is the receiver of such oral instructions (especially from a superior officer), it is often difficult or awkward to ask for a formal written order. In such a situation after carrying out the instructions, one should send a "compliance report" keeping a copy on one's own record and sending copies to the intermediate superiors, if any.

3. Government communications are issued in a variety of forms such as—

(a) ordinary letters
(b) demi-official letters
(c) memoranda
(d) Government Resolutions
(e) Notifications
(f) Orders
(g) Circulars
(h) Office-Memoranda
(i) Telegrams
(j) Press-notes and Press hand-outs
(k) Acknowledgment Cards.

4. The following characteristics of each of these, should be noted:

(a) **Ordinary letter:** This is used for most of the correspondence between Government offices or between a Government office and the public. In writing to the public one must be very careful about its wording and its legal implications. A mistake or indiscretion can be like a torch in the hands of a maniac.

When letters are used for commercial or legal transactions, care must be taken to see that these are supplemented by a proper legal contract or agreement.

The present writer is aware of a case in which a Government called for offers for the purchase of spoilt foodgrains in its godowns. (These are used for making cattle or poultry feed). Government then allotted quotas to all the applicants and asked them *by a letter* to pay some earnest money deposit, which they did immediately. One of the allottees however, failed to lift his quota but demanded the refund of his deposit contending that an ordinary letter could not constitute a contract which has to be executed "By order and in the name of the Governor" by an officer specifically authorised under Article 299 of the Constitution. The contention was upheld by the Legal Department and Government had to refund the deposit in full.

(b) **Demi Official letter (D.O. Letter):** This is a special type of letter written by one officer to another *by name* to invite his personal attention to an important or delayed matter. At one time demi-official letters were supposed to be written by officers of the same rank who knew each other personally. This convention has now broken down and demi official letters are often written on cyclostyled forms even by Section Officers to Collectors and Commissioners. With every officer receiving a dozen demi official letters every day, demi official letters have lost their sanctity and weight.

(c) **Memorandum:** This is a communication written by a higher office to a lower one. The only difference between a letter and a memorandum is that whereas a letter (to an office of superior or equal status), begins with "Sir", a memorandum (to a lower office) used to begin with a very ornamental expression—"The undersigned present compliments". An example of a memorandum has been given in para 3(5) of the next chapter.

These days many Government offices have discontinued this expression and a memorandum is now drafted just like a letter without "Sir" at the beginning.

(d) **Govt. Resolution:** This is a Government order sanctioning some scheme, rules, project or even expenditure in individual cases. Quite often it is supplemented by a statutory or legal notification or order. All resolutions, notifications and 'orders' are issued "By order and in the name of the President or the Governor".

(e) & (f) **Notification and Order:** These are usually statutory communications which are issued under the provisions of some Act or rule. In many cases drafts of these statutory instruments are required to be published to allow the public to record their objections or suggestions. In such cases, two precautions have to be taken—

(i) If the final notification differs radically from the original draft and especially if it affects any section of the public adversely, a revised *draft* notification has to be published again.

(ii) The public has to be given reasonable time to record their objections and suggestions.

(g) **Circular:** This is usually an advisory communication—often a supplementary explanation to a resolution, notification or order; but coming from a superior authority, it is as good as an order.

(h) **Office Memorandum:** This is either an order or an advisory circular to the office staff but is also sometimes circulated to lower offices which are supposed to circulate it to their staff.

(i) **Telegrams:** With teleprinters, fax and STD phones, the use of telegrams in Government is on the decline. However, Government telegrams are worth a study for their verbosity. They sometimes include even articles like 'a' 'an' or 'the' or entreating words like 'Please' and 'Kindly'.

(j) **Press-note and Press hand-out :** A press note is an official announcement meant to (i) communicate to the public either some new policy or scheme or programme of Government, or (ii) to explain the Government position with respect to any criticism or misunderstanding about Government policies or any incidents involving a Government department.

Press-notes refuting public criticism of Government should be issued as early as possible— if possible within twenty-four hours. Unfortunately in most cases such press-notes are issued after a week or a fortnight by which time the incident which gave rise to public criticism has gone out of public mind, but the unfavourable impression about Government inefficiency, indifference or slackness remains stuck in the public mind and cannot be wiped out by a press-note issued after a fortnight.

A Press-handout is an informal briefing to the press and not meant to be treated as an official announcement or explanation.

(k) **Acknowledgement Receipts:** In pre-Independence days Government departments were expected to acknowledge the receipt of every letter received from a member of the public. There used to be standard *printed* post cards which also provided space for writing the "inward" registration number under which the communication was registered in the office. This practice has more or less fallen into disuse because of the increased volume of work and the increase in postage charges. (The postage for a printed card is the same as for an in-land letter (75 paise).

5. The discontinuance of this practice has given rise to three undesirable consequences—

(i) The person who sends the communication is worried whether the letter has at all reached the Government office and goes on pelting the office with reminders which also remain unanswered. This gives rise to a feeling of neglect and indifference by Government. There is a general impression among common people that only letters sent through VIPs like MLAs, MPs and important political leaders are considered seriously.

(ii) If the matter is of sufficient importance, the poor applicant has to come all the way to the Government office to find out what has happened to his letter—sometimes travelling hundreds of miles from one end of the state.

(iii) When such a person arrives in a Government office or sends a reminder through a VIP, the office has to spend quite some time in tracing his letter.

6. The present writer once work-studied the Office of a Chief Minister where, after a new Chief Minister assumed office, there was very heavy accumulation of mail though all that the staff had to do was to enter each letter in a Register and pass it on to the concerned Secretariat department.

7. There were six clerks doing this work but they complained that half of their time was taken up by visitors coming to the office to find out what had happened to their letters. However, the office refused to implement the recommendation of the present writer to send printed acknowledgment cards to the applicants indicating the departments to which their letters had been forwarded.

8. Government Offices must, therefore, resume this old practice of acknowledging, at least the first letter, if not reminders. Government can also reduce the postage for Government acknowledgment receipt cards.

8

COMMUNICATION (2) : Principles of Drafting

Whatever the type of communication, it must conform to certain principles and methods of drafting. These principles of drafting are known by the acronym ABC, which stands for—

A – for Accuracy;
B – for Brevity; and
C – for Clarity.

2. One basic fact which must be borne in mind is that a communication is meant to send a message from a sender to a receiver. Therefore,

(i) the sender must be clear about what he wants to say;
(ii) the sender must bear in mind that the communication is meant for the receiver and must be worded taking into account the level of education and understanding of the receiver; and
(iii) there should be no scope for tampering or interference with the message at intermediate stages.

3. **Some Practical Hints:** The following nut and bolt rules should always be borne in mind in drafting all communications.

(a) The number and the date of the communication should be written very clearly at the usual place (right hand top corner for letters and in the case of Resolutions, Notifications,

Circulars in the middle, as shown below:

"Resolution of Government
No. ABC-23/5/B
15th April 1994"

(b) In the case of letters, the name (or designation) and address of the addressee should be written correctly at the top. Any mistake in this can result in the letter being misdirected.

(c) The subject of the communication is written just below the name and address of the party (in the case of Resolutions in the top right hand corner). There is a special way of writing subjects concisely which even many senior administrators are not aware of. Consider, for the example, the following two examples of subjects written by two senior colleagues of the present writer—

Sub:— Failure of Mr. XYZ to carry out ABC project according to contract.

or

Sub:— Visit of World Bank team to inspect the Narmada Project in August 1992.

The correct way to write the subjects in these cases is—

Sub:— ABC Project
failure of Mr. XYZ to carry out contract

Sub:— Narmada Project
visit of WB Team August 1992.

Written this way, the reader gets at a glance, what the communication is about.

(d) In the case of letters, and memos from other offices or private parties, the number and the date of the communication with reference to which the reply is being issued, should also be stated correctly. Any mistake in this respect can lead to waste of considerable time in searching for the letter at the receiver's end.

(e) In Government correspondence the number and date of the letter under reply is usually incorporated in the text of the letter as follows:—

> "Sir,
>
> With reference to your letter No. ABN–2460/C dated 23rd April 1989, on the subject mentioned above, I am directed to state etc...........".

One has to search for the reference through the body of the letter. This search becomes all the more difficult in an old style memorandum to a lower officer as in the example given below—.

> **"Memorandum**
>
> The undersigned presents compliments to the Controller of Textiles and with reference to his letter No. PQR 38/45-C dated 23rd January 1989, on the subject of the import of synthetic fibre from France, is directed to state that Government has decided that ...."

What a clumsy construction! but it is still being used in some offices. A much simpler way would be as follows:—

> Ministry of Industries,
> Udyog Bhavan,
> New Delhi-110 001.
> 20th March 1989.
>
> To,
> The Controller of Textiles
>
> Sub : Synthetic Yarn import from France
>
> Ref : Your letter No. PQR 38/45-CS dated 23/1/89.
>
> Government has decided that ....etc.
> ....
> ....
> ....
>
> (C.S. Bhargava)
> Under Secretary to Govt.

There is no reason why Government offices should not adopt this pattern of quoting subject and reference number and date separately at the top. For no other reason except blind adherance to habit, Government offices refuse to follow this method of quoting the reference.

4. Main Contents of the Communication

In the drafting of the main contents of a communication, the following rules should be kept in mind—

(1) Avoid long compound sentences. Break up such sentences into two or more short sentences.

(2) The letter should be divided into suitable paragraphs; each paragraph should usually deal with one point and should be numbered.

(3) Avoid ornamental expressions like—
"I have the honour to State....."
"I have to request you to be so good as to attend the meeting"

(4) Avoid superfluous or bombastic words and expressions like—

(a) "on the subject mentioned above"
(b) "The question has been under the serious consideration of Government which, after considering all the aspects of the problem, has decided ......"
(c) "I am not in a position to attend" (Just say I regret I cannot attend).

(5) Avoid superflous information or material which is not necessary for understanding a communication. Consider for example the following circular—

Circular

" I am directed to forward herewith a copy of letter No. 011/10/74-PS, dated the 9th August 1974 from the Government of Maharashtra on the subject mentioned above and to state that the question of implementation of the National Building Code in Maharashtra State was under the consideration of Government. In this regard an Implementation Conference on the National Building Code was held in Bombay on 28th August 1971 which passed two resolutions concerning the adoption of the Building Code by Government of Maharashtra and its bodies. An action Committee in its second meeting held on 5th April 1974 unanimously accepted the recommendations made in the National Building Code subject to minor variations as wanted by local bodies consistent with the principles of the National Building Code. In view of this position, I am directed to advise that the Municipal Corporations/Municipal Councils should modify their existing bye-laws, etc. to suit the provisions contained in the National Building code. For a copy of the National Building Code, which is a priced publication, the Director of Indian Standards Institution, Novelty Chambers, M. Shaukatali Road, Bombay-7, may please be approached."

2. The receipt of this letter may please be acknowledge and action taken in the matter may be communicated to Government early."

All the details about the various conferences held to consider the National Building Code etc. are unnecessary. The circular can be reduced to just three sentences as follows:—

Circular

"Government desires that the Municipal Corporations and Municipal Councils in the state should follow the provisions of the National Building Code. For this purpose, they should either frame new building bye-laws, or modify their existing bye-laws.
2. Copies of the National Building Code can be obtained from the Director, Indian Standards Institution, Novelty Chambers, Maulana Shaukatali Road, Bombay-400 007. "

(6) Avoid bombastic bureaucratic words like—
therein; therefor; apprise (instead of inform); render (give); transmit (send); endeavour (try).

(7) Use active instead of passive voice.

(8) Avoid vague instructions like—
(a) "Do the needful"—(A very common expression which really means "Do what you like. I don't know what is required to be done").
(b) "Submit relevant information."

In the first case tell the other office what exactly it is expected to do.

In the second case specify the items on which information is required preferably in an itemised form as follows:—

"Submit the following information :-

(i) the number of private primary schools in the town;
(ii) the total number of students in these schools;
(iii) the number of teachers in these schools;"

(9) When information to be collected is voluminous or is to be collected from a number of agencies, it is better to prescribe a tabular form. In the example cited above, if information is required separately for each school, a tabular form would be more convenient. However, where the information is only limited, the typing and filling of a form is often a waste of time (please see the form of 'Nil' return in Chapter 14.

(10) Orders should also be intemised as shown in item (8) above.

(11) Orders should as far as possible be self contained and should be understood without reference to previous orders. For example, if the rate of Conveyance Allowance is increased from the existing Rs. 200 per mensem to Rs. 300, do not say—

> "In Government Resolution No. CLA 1084 dated 12/3/84 for the figure '200' substitute '300'."

The receiving officer will not understand what this is about unless he sees the original order. The order in such cases should be worded as follows:—

> "Government has decided that with effect from 1st April 1992, the rate of Conveyance Allowance for Sanitary Inspectors in the Public Health Department should be increased from Rs. 200 to Rs. 300 p.m.
>
> 2. In para 4 of G.R. Public Health Department No. CLA-1084 dated 12/3/1984 for the figure "Rs.200" substitute "Rs. 300" with effect from Ist April 1992."

(12) When a Government Resolution or Order has undergone a number of amendments, it is better to replace it by a new self-contained order.

(13) Avoid the use of technical expressions excepts when dealing with another person conversant with such expressions. Expressions like *suo motu, locus standii* can convey much more than a whole paragraph but will be unintelligible to a common man. They can be used in correspondence between two lawyers or two high-level offices.

(14) Technical expressions can however, degenerate into jargon as can be see form the following example-

> "He has a top decile I.Q., an average rating in occupational involvement and low interpersonal competence".

In simple language this means—

> "He is a very intelligent person but does not take much interest in work and cannot get on well with other people".

Unfortunately, the use of this kind of jargon is on the increase especially in the reports of international institutions and their counterparts in this country.

(5) Correspondence Audit

Heads of large offices who cannot check all the communications going out from the office, can benefit from a system of correspondence audit in which copies of all the communications issued from the office are compiled in a file at the end of the day and sent to the Head of the office (or some senior officer if the Head is too busy). He then goes through all the communications.

This system is useful to the Head of the office in three ways:—

(i) He can check and improve some of the more serious drafting maladies of the type discussed in this chapter.
(ii) Second, it keeps him informed of cases not seen by him. (These days even replies to Legislature questions are issued without being shown to the Secretary.
(iii) Third, he becomes aware of cases which have been delayed badly.

(6) Legal Drafts

(i) Government offices hold legal drafts in great awe and usually leave the drafting of all legal instruments like bills, rules, notifications, orders etc. to the Law Department (or in the case of lower offices to some local lawyers). Whatever drafts are provided by these, are accepted as gospels.

(ii) Lawyers and Legal departments are more concerned with the wording of such laws and rules and less with their administrative implications which is the responsibility of the administrative office. Lawyers are also inclined to copy similar provisions from other Acts and rules, however clumsy they may be, because these have been interpreted by courts previously.

(iii) Administrative offices should, therefore, critically scrutinise drafts received from the Law Department or lawyers for their administrative implications. There is no need to be scared about legal drafts if you have been dealing with cases under these Acts. (The present writer had an Assistant who started as just a matriculate clerk but was better at legal drafting and interpretation than many law graduates).

9

OFFICE ORGANISATION

An organisation is a group of people working together to achieve a common object or objects. Though we sometimes talk of a "one-man organisation", essentially an organisation has more than one person to achieve a task which cannot be performed by a single person and we have to find an appropriate way of dividing work among the people.

Division of Work

2. There are four ways of dividing work—

(i) By Product or Subject,
(ii) By Process,
(iii) By Place or Territory,
(iv) By People or Clients.

These methods of dividing work can be best understood by the hypothetical example of a Stores-Purchasing Department which makes purchases on a large scale for all Government Departments. It deals with all kinds of stores including—(i) machinery, (ii) textiles, (iii) stationery, (iv) furniture and office equipment, (v) building materials, and (iv) other miscellaneous items. It gets indents from all the departments which can be divided into 5-6 groups. It receives indents from all parts of the country.

3. The work of this organisation can be divided in 4 different ways as shown in the charts in the Annexure IX-A to this Chapter.

(i) Chart I–By Product-*i.e.* the type of goods required.
(ii) Chart II–By Process-*i.e.* all the indents pass through all the

sections each performing a part of the procedure for processing the indent such as, (i) preliminary scrutiny, (ii) advertising, (iii) receiving and scrutinising of tenders, (iv) issuing final orders and making contracts, (v) inspecting goods, and (vi) watching payments.

(iii) Chart III—By Place or Territory-*i.e.* according to the area of the country or the states from which the indent is received.

(iv) Chart IV—By Clientele -*i.e.* according to the Departments for whom purchases are made.

4. There are no hard and fast rules to decide the best method of dividing work and one has to choose the method which is the most suitable. In general at higher policy making levels like the Secretariat, where one has to take an intergrated view of the whole subject including policy, programmes, budgets, personnel requirements as well as effect on other departments, division by Product (or Subject like Primary education, Secondary education or College education), is preferable. Where there is more routine or repetitive work, other methods are more suitable. For example—

(1) In a bank or in the Motor Vehicles Department the work is divided according to the account number or the vehicle number (Clientele Method).

(2) The work in the Public Works Department can be more suitably divided according to territory *i.e.* by districts or divisions.

(3) In a department dealing with purchases and supplies, a division by process as shown is Chart II may be more suitable.

5. One has to choose the method which is most suitable considering all factors. For example in the example of the Stores Purchase Organisation cited in Annexure IX-A, a Work-Study Officer suggested that a division by products as in chart I, would have been better as it would build up in each section, expertise about the class of goods (like electronics or textiles or stationery). The office however, informed the Work-Study officer that they had indeed an organisation divided on the basis of products (chart-I) but had changed over to an organisation based on process (chart-II) knowing full well that it was a less efficient method. Why?

6. The explanation given by the Office was that under a productwise division of work, an indent was under the control of one section at

all stages. Each section dealt exclusively with one class of suppliers and this often gave rise to unhealthy collusion between the suppliers and the section. This was undesirable in an organisation with dealings of crores of rupees. Therefore, even at the cost of some efficiency, they had chosen to change over to a process-based division of work (Chart II).

7. Whatever method we choose, it must be rational. Further, related subjects should always be grouped together. This would seem to be an obvious truth but one very often comes across serious breaches of it in Government Departments where new subjects are often allotted to sections with less pressure of work but without regard to the nature of the subject. This leads to fights and tossing of cases just to decide which section should deal with it.

Organisation Structure

8. The organisation of a department is usually in a pyramidal form as shown in Chart A and B below. (As we shall see later, there can be other alternative forms too).

The following points have to be taken into account in structuring an organisation :

(1) **Span of Control:** This is the number of subordinate employees supervised by one superior— whether a head clerk or a Deputy Director or a Secretary. Chart A and Chart B show two organisations with 32 clerks in each. In the first organisation (Chart-A), there are only 4 sections each with 8 clerks and 1 head clerk to superwise their work. Above the 4 head clerks there is only one Director. The span of each head clerk is 8 and that of the Director 4.

CHART - A

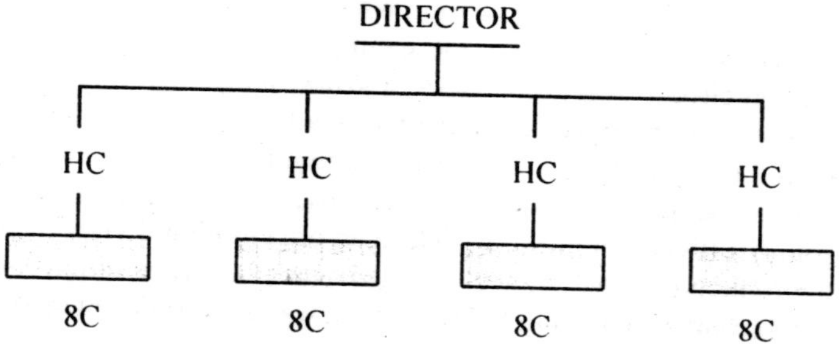

HC — Head Clerk; C — Clerk

CHART - B

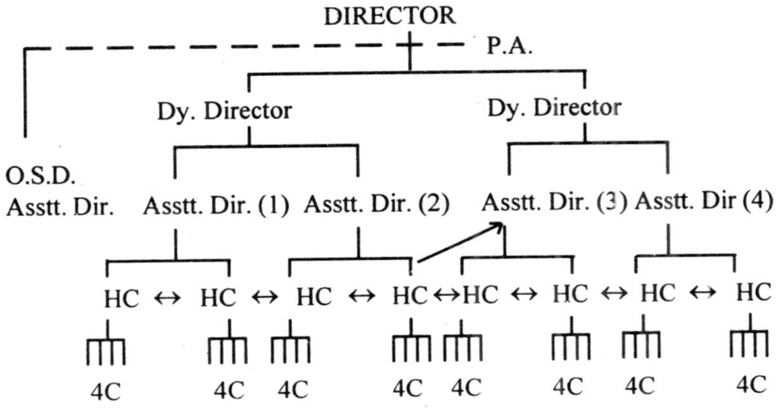

Sub - division in the field

In the second organisation (Chart B) there are 8 sections each with 4 clerks and 1 Head clerk to supervise their work. Above every two Head Clerks there is one Assistant Director. Above every two Assistant Directors, there is one Deputy Director and above the two Deputy Directors, there is one Director. The span of control of the Head Clerks is 4, while that of other officers is 2.

When the span of control is small, there is closer supervision of the subordinates which may not always be necessary and such over-supervision in some cases may be even harmful. There is, however, no ideal span of control which depends upon the nature of work. Where the work is routine and repetitive as in the case of a bank or a post-office counter, you can have a large span of control. In non-routine type of work, as for example in a policy-making organisation like the Secretariat, the span of control cannot be very large-not more than 4-5 Assistants per Section Officer.

One special case of span of control which should be avoided as far as possible, is a span of control of just one *i.e.* one supervisor with only one subordinate and *vice versa.* This is called a "one-over-one" organisation. In such an organisation the supervisor does not have sufficient work and starts creating work for the subordinate by raising unnecessary queries etc.

However, an exception to this general proposition is an office like that of an Executive Engineer in Maharashtra where there is only one

Deputy Engineer in the office of the Executive Engineer. *Prima facie* this looks like a "one-over-one" organisation; but it is not, because a large proportion of the Executive Engineer's duties consist of supervision of the work of Deputy Engineers in the field. His span of control, therefore, is not just one Deputy Engineer in the office but also the several Deputy Engineers in the sub-divisions in the field.

(2) **Hierarchy:** The organisation in chart A has only 3 levels while the one in chart B has 5 levels. These are called levels of hierarchy. It will be noticed that smaller the span of control, larger the number of hierarchical levels which makes decision making a slow process since every important case has to pass through and is often obstructed at more levels. It also demotivates the people at lower levels because of the delays in decision making. On the other hand, a large number of hierarchical levels (which means smaller span of control at all levels) give better scope for promotion and are welcomed by the staff.

One way of improving prospects of promotion without increasing the number of hierarchical levels is to introduce a system of selection grades within the same level. We do have selection grade Tehsildars, Dy. Collectors or senior and junior grade superintendents.

(3) **Line of Authority:** In both these charts, the top-most man is linked with the lowest clerk through a continuous line which is called the line of authority. All orders must always go down this line of authority which should never be broken. Similarly, cases going up for orders should always go up along the line of authority.

Senior officers are often tempted to establish a line of communication and authority with a bright subordinate two or three places below them on the hierarchical level ignoring intermediate superiors. This practice called "level-jumping" was once very popular but it is a very dangerous practice which not only keeps the intermediate officers in the dark but seriously demotivates them.

This level-jumping may be justified in some special cases when a senior officer dealing with some special work like the preparation of a report or scheme takes a lower level subordinate to assist him in that work for a short period.

(4) **Unity of Command:** Jesus Christ once said, "No man can serve two masters". If he does it as shown by a large arrow in Chart B where a Head Clerk is under the control of two Assistant Directors, No. (2) & (3), it is a violation of the principle of Unity of Command which requires that each employee should have only one superior or (in Management language) should report to only one superior. If this principle is violated, a subordinate can—

(a) either get crushed with orders (sometimes conflicting) from two supervisors; or

(b) can enjoy himself by playing off one supervisor against another.

Such situations often arise either because a superior complains about pressure of work or sometimes even out of considerations of economy.

In 1962 on the formation of Zilla Parishads in Maharashtra there emerged two parallel organisations in the districts—(i) the Revenue Department and (ii) the Zilla Parishad as shown below:—

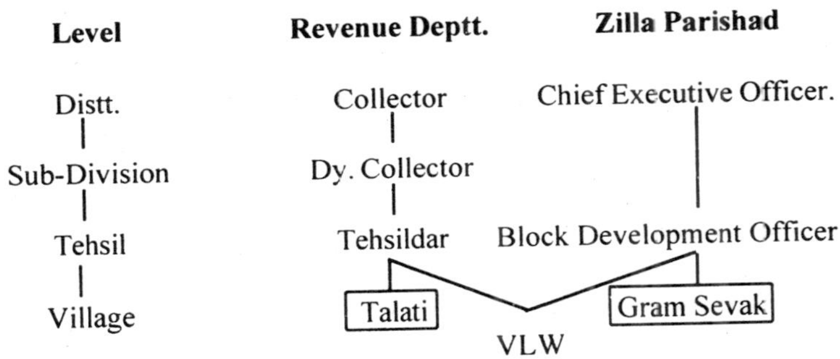

Government felt that it would be better to combine the offices of the Talati and Gram-Sevak into a single official in the village called Village Level Worker (VLW). This Village Level Worker found it difficult to work under two masters (viz. the Tehsildar and the B.D.O.) and after a few months the experiment had to be abandoned.

(5) **Gang Plank:** Although normally commands and communications in an organisation flow respectively down and up the lines of authority, there is no objection if information or communication (but not commands) are also allowed to flow side-ways as shown by small arrows (↔) between two Head Clerks in Chart B. This is called a gang-plank. (Gang-plank is a plank used by construction workers to move across horizontally along the face of a building).

(6) **Line and Staff:** All the posts in an organisation are usually on the lines of authority or hierarchy. There are, however, some posts which are not exactly on the main lines of authority as shown in Chart B. These are posts like those of Personal Assistants (P. As.) or Officers on Special Duty (OSD) which are usually fairly low-level posts but the incumbents of which report direct to fairly senior officers as shown by broken lines. Such employees are called "staff officers". They are usually not competent

to issue any orders but mostly assist the senior officer either by personal services (as in the case of a stenographer) or by expert advice (as in the case of Officers on Special Duty). Other officers on the regular lines of authority carrying out the orders of the superiors are called "Line Officers".

Such staff officers are useful to senior level officers—because (i) they relieve them of routine work, or (ii) they provide them with expertise or special information which normally a line officer would find difficult to collect. They thus help a senior officer to shoulder a much heavier burden of responsibility or expand his span of control and authority.

Staff officers, however, often create problems because of their special position in which, despite their low status, they have direct access to very senior level officers. A Personal Assistant to a Director often starts giving orders to the Deputy or Assistant Directors in the name of the Director. One remedy for this is to keep rotating officers between line and staff. Even stenographers should be rotated among officers.

(7) **Role Definition:** Whatever the division of work and the lines of authority, it is essential to be clear about the role of (*i.e.* the work or subjects allotted to) each worker and the superior to whom he is to report. For this job charts are very useful.

Likewise there should be for every table detailed *Job description files or charts* which list the various types of work or cases dealt with at the table and what action is to be taken on them. (See para 8 of Chapter 5).

(8) **Organisation Charts:** Every office should prepare organisation charts of the type shown in Chart-A and Chart-B. In the preparation of these charts the following precautions and conventions should be observed—

(i) The number of posts shown in the chart should be equal to the *sanctioned* number of posts.

(ii) Vacant posts, if any, should be shown in the charts—with the word 'vacant' written against them.

(iii) A common mistake in organisation charts is that if a section is submitting work to two different officers (in violation of the principle of Unity of Command), either the section or the officer is shown twice.

(iv) Posts of the same status should be shown at the same level.

(v) Lines of authority should be shown by continuous bold lines.

(vi) Staff posts like those of P.As should be shown by broken lines (see Chart B)

9. **Officer-oriented systems:** One alleged defect of the traditional Government organisations in India, is the preponderence of low level persons like clerks and assistants and a comparative deficiency of officers. A typical section in a Secretariat consists of 1 Section Officer or Superintendent, 3-4 assistants/senior clerks and 2-3 clerks. In most lower offices, we have senior clerks instead of assistants. The examination of a case starts at the level of an assistant (or senior clerk) and the case goes right upto the top through several levels of officers. The Section Officers, Head Clerks or Supervisors do not have the authority to take decisions on even the simplest cases such as calling for a report from a lower office on a routine complaint and the case has to be submitted to an officer before calling for a report.

To remedy this defect experiments with officer-oriented organisations have been tried in the Government of India and some State Governments. In one such experiment in the Maharashtra Secretariat, the old sections with 3-4 assistants and 2-3 clerks each, were broken up into very small sections called Desks each consisting of 1 Desk Officer, 1 Assistant and 1 clerk with half a typist (*i.e.* one typist shared by 2 Desks). There was also a stenographer or steno-typist for 3-4 Desks. The Desk officers were of the rank of either an Under Secretary or a Section Officer. All the Desk Officers had powers to take even final decisions on routine cases and to sign orders on behalf of Government on all cases-including even policy cases approved by Ministers.

The system is however, generally regarded as unsuccessful and has considerably reduced the efficiency of the Maharashtra Secretariat because of a number of inherent defects, in it, viz.—

(i) The very small sections split up each subject into small fragments which is very undesirable for an organisation like the Secretariat dealing with policy questions. An integrated view of a subject was available only at the level of the Deputy Secretary.

(ii) As explained in Chapter 3, the Memory function in a Government Office is very vital. The pool of 3-4 Assistants and 2-3 clerks under the old system assisted the retention and retrieval of office Memory. The small Sections made this difficult.

(iii) This organisation is what we have called a "one-over-one" type of organisation where each superior has only one subordinate under him—If one of them (particularly the Desk

Officer or the clerk) remains absent, the whole work of the section comes to a stand-still.

(iv) Stenographic assistance for Desk Officers was inadequate.

(v) In a typical section in a State Government Secretariat there are always a lot of petty cases which can be dealt with by Assistants and clerks. With just one Assistant, the Desk Officer had to deal with a large proportion of these routine cases without even adequate stenographic assistance. This was waste of an officer-level functionary on petty work.

(vi) Finally, the change was introduced all over the Secretariat at one stroke and in the wake of a prolonged strike of employees for nearly two months which had already dislocated work. (Organisational changes should never be made very lightly and should as far as possible be made gradually).

10. **Other Forms of Organisation** : The pyramidal hierarchical organisation discussed above, is also called the line and staff or the classical form of organisation because it has been used for several years especially in the armed forces and also by the Catholic Church which was, and still is, the most organised form of religion starting with the Pope at the top and going down to the smallest parish priest.

It is a somewhat rigid and mechanistic form of organisation like a machine where people are expected to behave according to a strict code of conduct depending upon their position--reporting to a single superior who is supposed to be more knowledgeable or at least more experienced than the subordinate. In the first part of the twentieth century, however, it came under attack on three grounds :

(i) The people at various points of this organisation are not mechanical parts but human beings with thinking capacities, emotions, sentiments, frustrations and fixations from earlier stages of life. Therefore, their reaction to any problem or situation differs from person to person. The psychological factors referred to above, can be an asset or a hindrance to the work of the organisation.

(ii) In addition to the formal relationship enjoined by the organisational structure, there are also informal relationships between people in different parts of an organisation created by religion, caste, language or even earlier working relationships within the organisation. These are sometimes more powerful than the formal relations stipulated by the organisational structure. For example, if a superior A asks a Section Officer 'B' to take some action against an Assistant 'C' in his section, B will try to thwart the order with the help of some superior officer M, if M, B and C all belong to the same community or caste. Instructions issued through such informal organisational channels are sometimes more effective than those issued through formal channels.

(iii) A rigid form of organisation is very often not suitable for all types of work specially non-routine or creative type of work or multi disciplinary work as in a scientific organisation or an advertising agency.

11. In recent years therefore many new types of organisations have been tried, a few of which are mentioned below :

(1) **Project Organisation :** In a project organisation persons from different disciplines are got together for a project and put in charge of a person who can at the most know just one of the many disciplines used in the project. Sometimes he may not be an expert in any subject but may be selected for his good managerial abilities. For example, a Superintending Engineer in charge of the construction a large hospital building may have under him besides engineers, an architect, a medical expert, an accountant and a social worker to advise him. The Superintending Engineer though superior to all these, may not know anything about these subjects. Such organisations are however, temporary and are disbanded after the project is over.

(2) **Matrix Organisation:** This is somewhat like a project organisation but more permanent. The Zilla Parishads in Maharashtra provide a good example of a matrix organisation as shown below:—

State Officer	ZP-A	ZP-B	ZP-C
	CEO	CEO	CEO
Dir. of Agrl.	Agrl. Officer	Agrl. Officer	Agrl. Officer
Dir. of Vet Services.	Vet.-Officer	Vet.-Officer	Vet.-Officer
Dir. of Education	Edn. Officer	Edn. Officer	Edn. Officer
Director of Accounts and Treasuries	Auditor	Auditor	Auditor

The officers in Zilla Parishads are deputed to Zilla Parishads from the respective Government Departments. They work under the Chief Executive officer but are also subject to the control of the Directors of their own departments especially regarding technical matters. They are thus subject to dual control (two masters) which is against the principle of Unity of Command of classical organisations but this is inevitable since each Zilla Parishad cannot have its own officers of the level of Directors.

The Command Area Development Administration (CADA) for irrigation projects is also a matrix organisation where officers from different departments like Agriculture, Irrigation, Public works, Co-operation and Accounts, work under a Superintending Engineer for the co-ordinated development of the command area of a project but are also subject to the control of their respective departments.

(3) **Free-Form Organisation:** In this form of organisation there is usually no fixed structure but people from different disciplines are pooled together for specific assignments. Advertising and publicity organisations, news papers and news agencies are sometimes organised in this manner. Newspapers pull out one or two correspondents and photographers from pools of correspondents and photographers and send them out for covering very hot events.

However, in Public Administration most organisations are line and staff organisations.

Common Defects of Government Organisations

12. Some of the most common defects and deficiencies of Government organisations are—

(1) A preponderence of low level workers like clerks and assistants and a comparatively small number of officers.

(2) Most of the recruitment is at the lowest level and there is very little intake of fresh blood at intermediate levels resulting in somewhat inward looking and stale organisations.

(3) Putting round pegs in square holes–or appointing people to posts without regard to their special aptitude and expertise, if any. This not only results in waste of talent but also demotivation of staff.

(4) Frequent transfers of officers which results in poor expertise at higher levels and, therefore, over-dependence on office.

(5) Lack of sufficient communication and interchangeability of office and field staff resulting in unrealistic policies and orders.

(6) Undue importance for seniority in promotions.

ANNEXURE IX-A

FOUR CLASSICAL WAYS OF DIVIDING WORK (IN A STORES PURCHASING DEPARTMENT)

1. According to Product or Subject

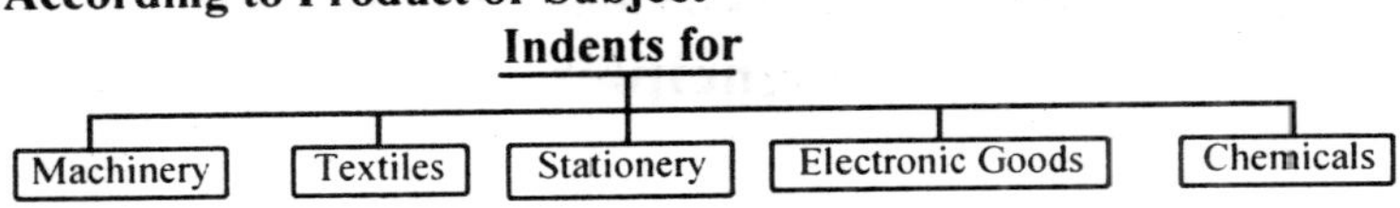

II. According to Process

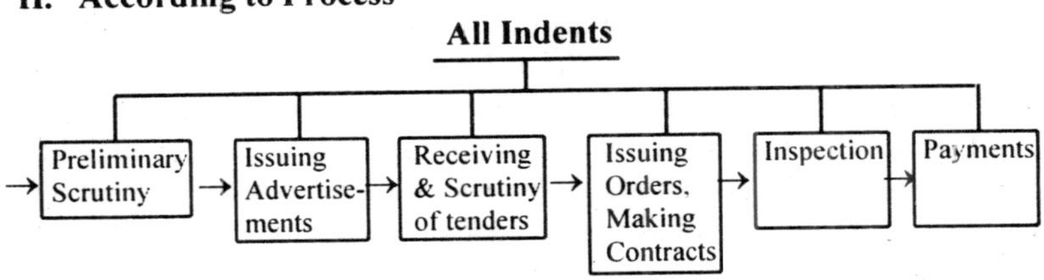

III. By Place or Territory

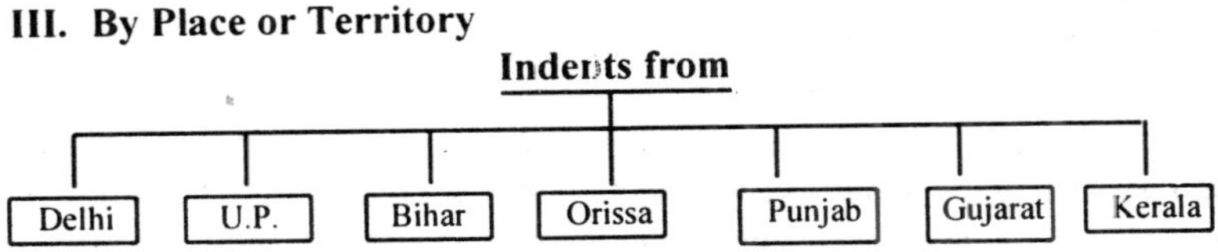

IV. By People or Clientele

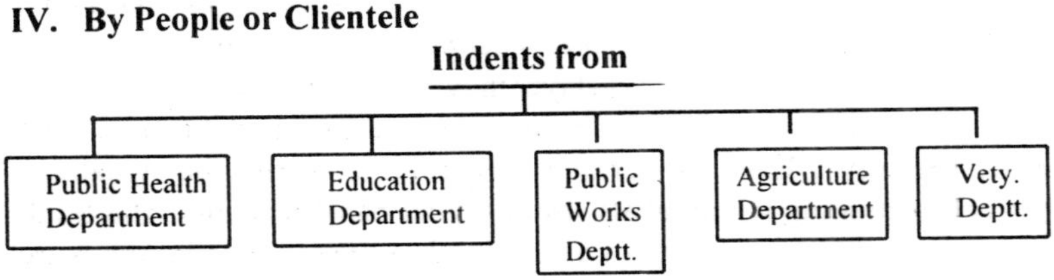

10

METHOD STUDY OR WORK SIMPLIFICATION (1) : Principles

The Science of Management started with the pioneering work-studies of Taylor and Gilbreth to improve the productivity of workers by improving the tools and methods of work, or by simplifying work. In modern industrial or business establishments where they have already attained very high levels of productivity and efficiency, they have been making more sophisticated "system" studies but in Government elementary work-studies are still very useful. Further, work simplification in Government is not just simplification of the mechanics of work but often requires a study and amendment of the relevant Acts, rules and circulars.

2. To start with, let us like Gilbreth think of a bricklayer building a compound wall [See Chapter 1]

He carries bricks and cement in two pans (called "ghamelas") which he keeps on the ground. Every time he lays a brick, he has to bend down at least twice–once to take cement and the second time to pick up a brick. This arrangement not only results in increased time per operation but also causes him considerable strain. If he were to keep the two pans on a small trolley, he can not only work faster but also avoid strain.

3. This example of a brick-layer may seem irrelevant for a Government office but we often work in the same manner in our offices. Just watch the way a Bank officer and a Post-master verify the signatures before sanctioning withdrawals from saving bank accounts. The Bank officer just pulls out a drawer of a cardex cabinet (See Fig. 3 in Annexure to Chapter 15) placed next to his elbow. He doesn't even have to get up from his seat. The whole operation does not take more than a minute. On the other hand, the Post-master has to get up from his seat every time,

search and then pull out a big register from a cupboard (usually about 4-5 feet from his seat), then search for the signature of the account holder in the register, verify the signature on the withdrawal form, again get up from his seat, walk back to the cupboard and keep the register back in the cupboard. The whole operation takes about four to five minutes. Isn't this like the bricklayer bending down every time to pick up bricks and cement?

4. Let us take another example. A Deputy Secretary in the Public Health Department of a State Government went on a short leave and another Deputy secretary was asked to handle his work for a couple of weeks. To his surprise and dismay, the latter found applications for casual leave from Honorary Medical Officers in some Government hospitals coming to the Secretariat. Having worked as an O&M officer before, he realised the futility and ridiculousness of the practice and immediately issued orders that these cases should be disposed of by the Hospital Superintendent himself.

5. When the other Deputy Secretary returned from leave, his locum mentioned to him what he had done and asked him why he had allowed this ridiculous and wasteful practice to continue. The other Deputy Secretary replied, "Oh it doesn't need even one minute to dispose of these cases. Why bother about them?"

6. What he did not realise was that while he had to spend only one minute per casual leave application, the total time lost was colossal because, the case had to come through the Hospital Superintendent, the Regional Deputy Director and the Director of Health. The case required the following action in each office.

(i) entry in the Inward Register	2 minutes.
(ii) entry in the Section Register	2 minutes.
(iii) drafting a letter	10 minutes.
(iv) typing and comparing it	10 minutes.
(v) submission to the officer for signature	2 minutes.
(vi) entering in the dispatch and delivery registers	2 minutes.
(vii) despatch it to the next office.	5 minutes.
	33 minutes

7. When the orders of Government were received, all these stages had to be repeated downwards. The total time lost on the case was nearly 264 minutes (or about 4-1/2 hours) plus the time for delivery which depends on a number of other factors like the distances between offices,

whether the letter was sent by hand delivery or by post and whether it was sent separately or bunched with other letters.

8. Now each Government hospital in Bombay has about 40-50 honorary medical officers and each officer applies for casual leave at least five to six times in a year. Imagine the volume of work which would have been generated if all the hospitals in the state were to follow this practice. You would probably need a separate Secretariat department to deal only with causal leave applications of Medical officers. (Fortunately this practice was being followed by just one or two hospitals).

9. Two questions arise. The first is how do such ridiculous practices arise? The answer is provided by the story of "Czarina's Violet" in some old school text-books. Several centuries ago, a young Czar of Russia went out for a stroll outside his capital city (Petrograd) which was probably then a small town with just a few thousand people. On the outskirts of the city, he saw a sentry standing guard in a desolate spot where there was nothing to guard.

10. Getting curious, he made enquiries about why the sentry had been posted there. No one seemed to know. Ultimately after a lot of enquiries and search of records it was discovered that decades ago, the young Czar's grandmother had once similarly gone out for a stroll and had found at that particular spot, some small bushes with beautiful violet flowers. She ordered that these flowers should be sent to her palace every day. So immediately a sentry was placed to guard the plants. In due course, the Czarina died, the bushes withered but the sentry continued to stand guard at the spot.

11. This is just what happens in our work. For some valid reason we start a practice but continue it even after the underlying reasons disappear.

12. One can find any number of such practices which have outlived their original justification. During the Salt Satyagraha of the thirties, the then Government of Bombay asked all the Tehsildars to submit a report every month about the number of cases of illegal manufacture of salt in their tehsils. Like Rip Van Winkle, one Tehsildar continued to submit a 'nil' return right upto 1960. When his Collector asked him why he had been submitting these returns, he replied that he was not aware of any orders for discontinuing the return. (Fortunately this return did not involve much work for the whole system like the casual leave applications of Honorary Medical Officers.)

13. The second question that strikes us is, why did the ridiculousness and superfluity of the practice strike one Deputy Secretary but not the other? The explanation is that the Second Deputy Secretary was a

trained O&M Officer who had developed the habit or out look of looking at work in a rational manner. The development of this *approach* or outlook is more important in O&M work than the techniques explained in books on O&M.

14. This approach is represented by the following questions which one should always keep on asking oneself not only in the office but in every walk of life:

O & M Approach

What is being done?	Why is it being done?	What is achieved? Is it necessary?

If it is necessary,

How is it done?	Why that way?	Is there a better way of doing it?
Who does it?	Why that person or Department?	Can it be done better by any other person or Department?
Where is it done?	Why there?	Can it be done better at any other place?
When is it done?	Why then?	Can it be done better at any other time?

These are called the 5 'W's of O&M (There is also one 'H'). With the help of these, we can simplify many cumbersome procedures of work.

There are also some more supplementary questions given below:—

(i) Can we combine something?
(ii) Can we standardise something?
(iii) Can we substitute something?

15. There are also some charting techniques like process charts, flow-process charts, flow diagrams used in this work. Some of these have been shown in Annexure 10-A to this chapter but they are not as useful as the approach explained above and the method of recording procedures shown in the Annexures to Chapters 3 and 13.

16. It should be noted that these questions fall into two parts-viz. (a) What, and (b) How, Who, Where and When. If the reply to the first question *i.e.* "What" is in the negative, we just eliminate or discontinue the particular activity and do not have to proceed to the next four or the supplementary questions. The two examples of casual leave for Medical

Officers or the periodical return about illegal manufacture of salt fall into this category of work which can be eliminated totally.

17. The items of work which can be totally eliminated are however, not many; and for the remaining items of work we have to proceed to the other questions and see how the work can be simplified. The Postmaster's job of tallying the signatures of account holders can be simplified by the use of a cardex-cabinet.

18. In the next chapter we shall give more examples of work-simplification.

ANNEXURE 10 A

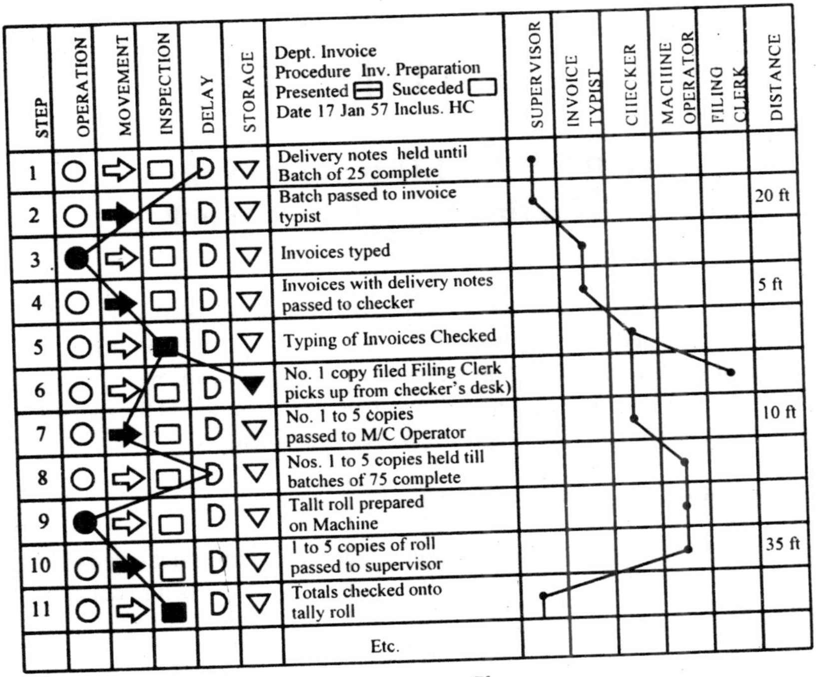

Flow Process Chart

11

WORK SIMPLIFICATION (2) : Eliminating Superfluous Work

1. We shall now see some more examples of work simplification from actual work-studies. As stated in the last chapter, work simplification falls into two parts—(i) Elimination of unnecessary work by using the first "W" "What" and (ii) Rationalisation or simplification of the remaining work by the use of How, Who, Where and When.

Elimination of Unnecessary Work —

What is being done? Why is it being done? What is achieved? Is it necessary?

Examples

(1) **Court Fee Refunds:** When a court case is compromised or settled amicably, the court orders a refund of a part of the court fee. We found that orders of such refunds from the Bombay High Court were sent to the Stamp Office for counter-signature of the Superintendent of Stamps. There were about 20-25 cases per day being sent from the High Court to the Stamp Office for counter-signature. All this meant a delay of 3-4 weeks in making refunds apart from additional work created in the Stamp Office. Further, it was found that while all the lower courts like the Small Causes Court and the City Civil Court were sanctioning refunds without counter-signature of the Stamp Office, the High Court was not competent to do so. No satisfactory explanation was available for this anomaly.

The Stamp Office could not recall a single case where they had modified or objected to a refund sanctioned by the High Court. The counter-signature of the Stamp Office was a mere routine formality like stamping letters in post offices. After discussion the Stamp Office agreed to discontinue the system with the approval of the High Court.

(2) The Director of Industries in Maharashtra recommends the allotment of certain categories of raw materials in short supply to small scale industries. One such commodity was coal. The Directorate used to receive applications from hundreds of small-scale industries for coal. The Inspectors of the Directorate used to visit each factory to verify its need for coal. One very capable Director who tried to examine the working of this system, discovered that the Coal Control Order which gave rise to this huge work had expired some years back.

This example high-lights the importance of examining Acts, rules and orders in simplifying work in Government.

(3) For many examinations for clerical posts, the Public Service Commission receives thousands of applications. Formerly, each applicant was required to attach to the application form, his *original* certificates of having passed the qualifying examinations (either the school leaving or the degree examination). All these certificates were examined by the staff, before admitting a candidate for the examination and then returned to the candidate by *registered* post. It involved huge clerical work and expenditure on postage and also led to long delays in holding examinations. The scrutiny of the certificates of candidates who did not ultimately qualify, was just a waste of time labour and money. So at the suggestion of a work-study team the Commission introduced a new system under which it dispensed with this preliminary scrutiny of original certificate. Only candidates who qualified (these numbered just a few hundred) were asked to produce their original certificates. That eliminated nearly 90 per cent of the work of receiving, scrutinising and returning the certificates (by registered postage) and reduced the delays in holding examinations.

(4) Often the lack of standardisation creates avoidable work.

In one department with a large number of educational institutions under it, there was a flood of work about the refund of fees to students who leave institutions in large numbers at the beginning of the year—mostly on account of getting admission to a better course or institution. The institutions would refer each application for refund to the Director of the Department for orders. It was a new Department which had just started expanding. It had a number of new institutions and had no policy or rules about refund of fees. The Director's Office would, therefore, refer each case for advice to one of the oldest institutions under the Department. This old institution would then tell the Directorate how much refund they sanctioned in such a case. The Director's office would then instruct the Principal of the new institution to make a refund accordingly.

All this was useless work which occupied almost the whole time of one clerk for nearly two to three months. No one had ever thought of eliminating all this by making standard rules for refund for all the institutions till a work-study team visited the office and pointed out the need for such rules.

(5) Maharashtra has about 250 Municipalities and a State cadre of Chief Officers. Often, there are vacancies in this cadre which are filled temporarily by deputing officers of the Revenue Department. Government used to issue two orders—(i) an order just appointing the officer issued by the Urban Development Department, and (ii) a second order laying down the terms of deputation of the officer issued by the Revenue Deptt. The first order had to be issued immediately as otherwise the officer could not take charge of the appointment. The second order, however, used to take months because it involved consultation between (i) the Urban Development Department in charge of municipalities, (ii) the Revenue Department, from which the officer was deputed, (iii) the General Administration Department in charge of services, (iv) the Finance Department dealing with the rules of deputation (v) the Divisional Commissioner and sometimes even the Collector (in the case of non-gazetted officers).

The procedure involved a minimum 10 steps as follows:—

(1)	Urban Development Department.	—	asked the Revenue Department to issue orders about the terms of deputation.
(2)	Revenue Department	—	asked the Divisional Commissioner to submit proposals.
(3)	Divisional Commissioner	—	wrote to the Collector.
(4)	Collector	—	wrote back to the Commissioner proposing terms of deputation.
(5)	Commissioner	—	submitted the terms to the Revenue Department.
(6)	Revenue Department	—	sent the case to—
(7) & (8)			(a) Urban Development Deptt. (b) General Administration Deptt. (c) Finance Department.
(9)	Finance Department	—	returned the case to the Revenue Department.
(10)	Revenue Department	—	issued orders.

If any Department raised an objection at any stage, there was an increase in the number of steps and the time required for the final orders.

This process of consultation used to take more than six months and the deputed officers usually could not get their salaries for several months.

A new Deputy Secretary with some work-study experience found that the orders of deputation terms issued in all the cases were more or less identical except for the name of the officer and the municipality. He therefore issued a general order laying down the *normal* deputation terms whenever any officer is sent on deputation. Special orders were necessary only for exceptional cases. This not only eliminated the second order but also eliminated a very great source of hardship for the officers.

(6) Offices sometimes continue to do useless work knowing full well that it is useless. One department had given loans to hundreds of displaced students from Pakistan after Independence. In 1965 a work study team found that the department had about 100 files each dealing with the case of a "student" who had not repaid the loan and who was not traceable.

Every year the department would take out the 100 files from the cup-board, and write to the Collectors of the districts to trace the students and recover the amounts as arrears of land revenue (The Collectors have drastic powers to recover any Government dues as arrears of land revenue). After about a month or two, each Collector would report that the 'student' was not traceable nor did he have any property which could be attached. This ritual had been going on year after year. Apart from the clerical correspondence there was also the work of trying to trace these 100 "students" which involved the whole Revenue Deptt. down to the village level.

When a work-study officer suggested that the Department should write to the Police Department, make one serious effort to trace the missing 'students' and, if the Police Department also failed to locate the "student", write off the loans with the sanction of Government and close the files. The reply given by the office was that this remedy would be worse than the disease because if the loans were written off, it would appear in the audit report and that would be the signal for a big enquiry. It was much better to continue this pantomime show of going through the motion of trying to recover the loans.

(7) **Periodical Returns:** This is another item that creates a huge volume of useless work. Government Departments are in the habit of prescribing a return at the drop of a hat. There are often three or four returns on the same subject-monthly, quarterly, six-monthly and annual. In one Department with multifarious activities the Divisional offices were required to submit nearly 200 returns to the Head of the Department.

After nearly one month of study we were able to reduce them by 50 per cent.

(8) In the last chapter we came across a Rip Van Winkle-like Tehsildar submitting a return about illegal manufacture of salt. That however, was an innocuous return which did not create much work. Other instances are not so harmless. The Department of Agriculture in Maharashtra used to collect from nearly 250 Tehsildars, monthly returns about prices of about ten essentials commodities, enter them in a register, prepare huge statements (250 ×10) and send them to the Press (usually after a year or two) for publication in the Government Gazette. More than 50 per cent of the entries in the statement were blank because the Tehsildars were very irregular in the submission of the returns. A concurrent study at the Government Press revealed that the cost of printing these statements in the Gazette was nearly Rs. 60,000 per annum (in 1965; today it would be about Rs. 3-4 lakhs).

The Department could not indicate what use was being made of these statistics which were being compiled from pre-War days.

The compilation of these crude statistics which were based on information gathered in a very unscientific manner, was probably justified in an era when Government had no other machinery to collect such information. Today information about prices is being collected more systematically by the Labour Department, the Department of Economics and Statistics and some other agencies like the Indian Statistical Organisation. There was no need for the Department of Agriculture to collect such statistics which were discontinued.

(9) Many Government returns are wasteful because they seek to collect too much information a large proportion of which is useless. As stated above, Maharashtra has nearly 250 municipalities. The Department of Economic and Statistics used to collect statistics about municipalities which were consolidated and printed in a huge book about 1 square metre in size. The collection of such information from 250 municipalities and its consolidation used to take a long time so there was a delay of nearly 4-5 years between the date of these statistics and their publication. They were useless for any decision making. The Urban Development Department therefore introduced a very small return of just 4-5 fulscap size pages and the information was collected, consolidated and published within a year (even without the use of computers).

(10) A large proportion of returns received by Departments are "nil" returns but the reporting office has still to type an elaborate form and then write "nil" in it. In the sixties the Government of Maharashtra on the recommendation of a work-study team, introduced a post-card for such "nil" reports on the following lines:

> To
>
> Sub.: Return re
> G.C. No. dated
> Period:
>
> So far as this office is concerned the above return is "nil".
>
> Signature.

This saves postage as well as typing time. However this return has now fallen into disuse. That is the fate of many good innovations.

12

WORK SIMPLIFICATION (3) : Delegation

Delegation is a very effective way of simplifying work. It also results in reduction of work in higher offices but not its total elimination from the system as in the case of price-statistics. It also quickens decision making. We shall see two examples of delegation :

(1) **Recovery of Rationing Department Dues :** The Rationing Department of Maharashtra buys foodgrains from the Food Corporation of India (FCI) and distributes it through Authorised Ration shops or Fair Price shops. When the FCI increases the price of its foodgrains, the Rationing Department has to increase the sale price to the shops which in turn have to increase the sale price to the customers. All these three increases come into effect on one common day (let us call it the 'D' day).

On the D-day the shopkeeper has some stock issued by the Rationing Department prior to revision as well as new stock issued at the revised price. From the D-day the shopkeeper has to sell both these at a common price, the revised enhanced price. He has, however, to pay to Government the difference between the old and the new price in respect of the old stock.

For this purpose, after the closure of business on D-1 day, the Inspectors attached to each Ward Office in Bombay used to visit the shops and make an inventory of the stock in each shop, enter the information in a form and send it to the Head Office of the Controller of Rationing. There were about 40 Ward offices under the Controller, about 20-25 Inspector for each Ward office and about 25 shops per ward — in all nearly 2000 shops. The office of the Controller of Rationing thus used to receive about 2000 forms at the time of every revision showing the old stock in each shop. It used to calculate the amount payable by each shopkeeper, get it checked from the Chief Accounts Office (an independent office situated at some distance from the office of the Controller of Rationing) and then issue a notice to each shopkeeper to pay the amount due.

There were about 2000 shops in Greater Bombay and the whole process used to take such a long time that even though in 3 years there had been five or six revisions, the calculations had been completed and checked in respect of only *one* revision. Notices were still to be issued to the shopkeepers. The total amount recoverable in respect of this one revision for which calculations had been made, was nearly Rs. 5 lakhs; so the total amount recoverable for five or six revisions would have been about Rs. 25-30 lakhs. Not one paisa had been recovered in these 3 years.

A work study team therefore, suggested that the inventory forms prepared by the Inspectors should be returned to the Ward offices. The Inspectors should calculate the amounts and after a check by the Ward Rationing Officer, issue notices to the shopkeepers to make payments making it clear in the notice that the amounts stated in the notices were liable to revision after they were checked by the Chief Accounts Officer. Despite some resistance, the suggestion was accepted and implemented and the whole amount of Rs. 25-30 lakhs was recovered within about 4-5 months.

This is an example of delegating power and functions to a lower offices. It eliminated the work from the Head Office but not from the whole system.

(2) A certain department had a large number of post–S.S.C. educational Institutions. There used to be one merit scholarship at each institution for each class. The whole work of awarding scholarships had unnecessarily been centralised in the Director's Office which used to create a special Section every year for about 6 months for the award of these scholarships. The result of the centralisation was that the scholarships were usually sanctioned almost at the end of the year and were of no use to the needy students.

There were about 9-10 scholarships per institution — one for each class. There were about twenty to thirty institutions so that the total number of scholarships was about 200-300. The principles for the award of each scholarship were simple. It was to be awarded to the student who had stood first at the last annual examination provided his parents' income was less than Rs. 450 p.m. (in the sixties). The student had to produce a certificate from an officer of Government about the income of his parents. (If the income was more than Rs. 450 p.m. the student was only awarded a certificate of having qualified for the scholarship but the scholarship amount was awarded to the next eligible student. The work could have been delegated to the Principals but the office needed a lot of persuasion and argument before it could agree to the suggested delegation.

General Observations

3. In theory people always talk enthusiastically about the need to delegate but in practice when it comes to delegating one's own powers, every conceivable objection is raised. Often powers delegated to the lower officers are withdrawn on the slightest pretext–may be a mistake made by a subordinate. So it would be useful to set down the principles of delegation.

- (i) Powers should be delegated to the lowest possible level near the point of action. The capability of the officers at the level should always be kept in view.
- (ii) The authority delegated should be commensurate with the responsibility of the subordinate.
- (iii) The delegation must be clear, specific and in writing, but there should be some flexibility.
- (iv) Delegation of authority to a subordinate office or officer does not absolve the superior office or officer of his own responsibility for the work. He has got to check and inspect from time to time the way the subordinate exercises the power, without breathing down his neck all the time. At the same time, it must be borne in mind that the subordinate is bound to make some mistakes. One must then try to help him but if he persists in making mistakes, the power may have to be withdrawn or the subordinate transferred to another post.

4. There is often a tendency on the part of the subordinate offices to avoid using the powers delegated but submit the cases to the superior. Many superiors welcome such dependence by the subordinates.

5. Two special characteristics of delegations in Government may be noted—

- (1) Delegation in Government is always institutional or to a class— and not to individuals. A power or authority is delegated to all the Collectors or all the Tehsildars and not to any individual Collector, however, brilliant or capable he may be. (In the private sector, delegations are often personal according to the capacity and experience of the individual).

(2) A large part of delegation is in terms of financial powers ... e.g. authority is given to a class of officers to purchase stores locally upto Rs. 10,000 in a year; or create a temporary post for 1 year not involving an expenditure of Rs. 3000 per month. In an age of rapid inflation, these limits get eroded and no attempt is made to bring them in line with the price level. After four or five years Government (usually the Finance Department) takes up the question of revising the limit but never restores it to its original value in terms of the purchasing power of the rupee.

6. To cite two concrete instances, in 1888 the Municipal Commissioner of Bombay had powers to finalise contracts upto Rs. 15,000. Considering the purchasing power of the Rupee then, this would be equivalent to about Rs. 25,00,000 today; but the Municipal Corporation Act was not amended till 1984 when the limit was raised to Rs. 5 lakhs. So even after amendment, the limit of purchasing power of the Commissioner was about one-fifth of what it was in 1888.

7. In the other Municipal Corporations including Pune, governed by the Bombay Provincial Municipal Corporations Act, 1949, the original limit laid down in the Act was only Rs. 5,000 and has still not been revised though the prices have risen more than 10 times since then.

8. In the present era of inflation, Government should issue before the beginning of each year a fresh order revising the financial limits of delegation — just as they revise the limits of exemption for income tax or the rates of dearness allowances.

A still better method would be for Government to fix *before the beginning* of each year, a multiplier and leave it to the offices to work out the new limits of financial powers by multiplying the limits in the original order by the multiplication factor.

13

WORK SIMPLIFICATION (4) : Improving Procedures

1. The items of work which can be eliminated from an office are limited — not more than 10-20 per cent. For the remaining work there is plenty of scope for rationalising and simplification and doing it more economically and efficiently and we do this with the help of the other 4 questions *viz.* HOW, WHO, WHEN and WHERE. It should be noted that these are not independent questions but often interlinked. Some examples of such simplification are given below.

(1) Our police-stations have to file and fight a large number of cases in courts. When the judgments are received, copies have to be prepared and sent to different offices. Till recently, the police-stations in Bombay used to do this work manually with the help of constable-writers who used to copy the judgments by hand. There were about 800 constable-writers in the Department. This ridiculous practice came to light during the course of Zero-Base budgeting studies. The department was supplied with 40 copying machines which released nearly 800 constable-writers for regular police duties. The cost of 40 machines would be about Rs. 20 lakhs *(non-recurring)* whereas the *recurring* expenditure on nearly 800 constables was estimated at Rs. 1.21 crores. At the present rates of pay and allowances the expenditure would be nearly Rs. 2.5 crores recurring.

(2) Many offices like the Sales Tax Department, the Public Service Commission, the Magisterial Branch of the Collector's Office have to receive a large number of applications or returns. These

are accepted at a counter without examination and sent to the office which scrutinises them after a lapse of time — (sometimes as much as a few months). Some routine omissions such as failure to attach a challan or a certificate are communicated to the party after some months. This creates considerable correspondence work and gives rise to delays.

All this can be avoided by strengthening the receiving counter-clerks both quantitatively as well as qualitatively and carrying out the preliminary scrutiny at the counter before accepting the application or return. If it is not complete, the counter-clerk should return it to the applicant explaining to him the omissions.

It may be noted that here we are changing the time (when), the place (where) and the person (who) doing the work of preliminary scrutiny and in the process we also change the method (how).

2. Quite often work-simplification is not as simple as this-just changing the time or/and the place of work but one has to study and change the whole system; and ideas of work simplification often flash like a "gestalt" in psychology. Here are two examples –

(1) **Rain-gauge Stations :** Maharashtra has nearly 400 rain-gauge stations where a rain-guage is kept either in the compound of a school or post-office or village chavdi. The equipment consists of : (i) a small metal cylinder closed at one end and with a conical funnel of standard size at the other. There is a small container or beaker below the funnel which collects rain-water falling into the funnel. The equipment is in charge of some local official like a school-teacher or post-master who from time to time removes the beaker and measures the water collected, with the help of a standard measuring glass, records the rain and reports it to the Director of Agriculture.

The equipment or parts of it often get damaged or stolen and the officer-in-charge asks for replacement through the Tehsildar who writes to the Director of Agriculture who used to get the equipment from a Government Scientific Instruments factory in Calcutta. It was noticed that this process of replacement used to take months and sometimes even a year or two during which period the rain-gauge station remained inoperative. The progress of a typical case is given in Annexure 13A at the end of this chapter. After studying a few such cases, a Work-study officer suggested that the Director of Agriculture should create a small central depot in Poona, stock this equipment and supply it to the Tehsildars, instead of sending each indent to Calcutta separately.

Readers should note the format in which this typical case has been presented in the Annexure. It brings out clearly the stages at which delays take place. This method of presentation is somewhat similar to the process charts used in work-studies of mechanical work, and is better than a simple narration as given in Annexure 13-B.

Care has to be taken that the case so selected is a typical case and not an exceptional one. If time permits, select about ten cases at random and take the average time required for each stage, though, in Government Offices with a large variety of problems, it is sometimes not possible to be so statistically sophisticated.

(2) **Rent Recovery Procedure:** The Maharashtra State Government has a large number (about 2000 in 1965) of residential tenements in Bombay which are let out to Government employees scattered over several offices. The rent charged is equal to 10 per cent of the salary *plus* some service charges. The employee does not pay the rent in cash but it is deducted through his salary bill.

The Executive Engineer in charge of the tenements used to send every month to the office of every employee occupying a Government tenement, a form called a "rent-roll" in which the office was asked to report to the Executive Engineer the pay of each such employee and the amount deducted through the salary bills. About 1500 rent rolls were required to be sent every month. Most of the offices failed to return these forms and so the clerks from the office of the Executive Engineer used to visit the various offices spread over the city and collect the rent-rolls personally. With all this effort they could collect rent rolls in respect of only about 30-35 per cent of the tenements. This created two problems :

(i) It gave the impression of huge arrears of rent though in reality, practically all the rent was being collected through the pay bills.

(ii) Many employees who had been paying rents regularly, used to receive ultimatums from the Executive Engineer's office to pay up huge arrears of rent or to vacate the premises. They had then to get a certificate from their office about rent recovered through the pay bills, produce it before the Executive Engineer and get the notice cancelled.

As the offices did not care to return the rent-rolls, the Public Works

Department decided to put the onus of reporting recovery on the employees concerned and directed that every allottee should obtain a certificate from his department about the recovery of rent and send it to the Executive Engineer.

The earlier rent rolls were not discontinued; so the Executive Engineer's office was supposed to receive 1500 rent rolls from office cashiers plus 2000 certificates sent by individual employees—in all about 3500 pieces of paper per month. In practice even the individual allottees turned out to be as lax as office cashiers and there wasn't much improvement in the recording of recoveries. The problem was, therefore, handed over to a work-study team.

The work study team noticed that there were three reports about the recovery— (i) the rent roll and (ii) the certificate sent by the allottee from the Department to the executive Engineer and (iii) a rent recovery certificate (called "schedule") going to the Pay and Accounts office with the pay bill, which sent it on to the Accountant General. The position is shown by the diagram below :

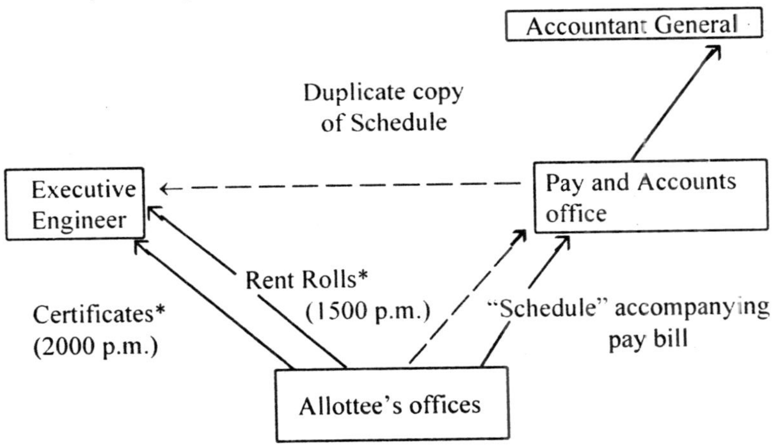

(* Eliminated in revised procedure:)

_ _ _ _ Duplicate copy of schedule introduced in the revised procedure.

The allottee's office did not care much about the rent roll and the certificate but could not ignore the schedule. If it failed to attach the 'schedule' to the pay bill, the pay-bill was promptly returned to the office. There was thus an element of *compulsion* about this "schedule".

The work study team decided to take advantage of this compulsion.

It recommended the abolition of the rent-rolls and the certificates and suggested that the schedules (which needed some slight modification) should be submitted to the Pay and Accounts Office in duplicate and one copy of it should be sent by the Pay and Accounts Office to the Executive Engineer. The rent-rolls and certificates were abolished, reducing the volume of papers received in the Executive Engineer's office.

Some difficulty was experienced because of the reluctance of the Pay and Accounts Office to detach the schedules and send them to the Executive Engineer. This was solved by giving the clerks in the Pay and Accounts Office some monetary incentives linked with the number of schedules they detached and sent to the Executive Engineer's Office.

The record of recoveries in the Executive Engineer's Office went up to more than 90 per cent.

Importance of Study of Acts Rules etc.

3. As stated earlier, many complicated or wasteful procedures arise out of faulty provisions of Acts, rules, circulars etc. and a study of these is often very rewarding. Here are a few examples:

(1) **Registration of Small-scale Industries:** Small-scale industries registered with the Directorate of Industries in Maharashtra are entitled to receive certain facilities and concessions. The process of registration was however, a very harrowing experience with several forms., inspections and queries. A dynamic Director of Industries once went through the complicated procedure and found that there were as many as 97 circulars issued from time on the subject, some of them even conflicting with each other. Most of these circulars and instructions had been received from some organisations in Delhi and had been passed on by the State Government to its officers.

The Director himself analysed all these circulars with the help of his officers and reduced them to one single circular setting down in a neat and concise form the minimum requirements for registration.

(2) **Publication of Municipal Rules and Bye-laws :** Under the Maharashtra Municipalities Act, before any rules or bye-laws were adopted by a municipality, it had to publish a draft of such rules or bye-laws in a news-paper circulating in the municipal area. Most municipalities used to publish these drafts (which often covered a whole page of a news-paper) in some prominent paper like the Maharashtra Times with a circulation of more than a lakh *all over the state*. This involved expenditure

of thousands of rupees per advertisement which was sheer waste because out of the lakhs of readers of the paper only a few people in the municipal area were likely to be interested in the rules or bye-laws.

A new Deputy Secretary with some work-study background, immediately got the Act amended to provide that the Municipality shall only publish a *small* notice in a newspaper that the draft rules or bye-laws were available for sale or inspection at the municipal office. This resulted in savings of lakhs of rupees.

(3) **Condonation of Marks :** A certain Directorate in Maharashtra holds a large number of examinations for diplomas. After the results of every examination, Government used to receive a large number of applications (about 150) from students who had failed—

(a) either requesting Government to condone their failure on compassionate grounds; or
(b) complaining about unfair practices in granting condonation.

The Director's office complained that the Secretariat unnecessarily entertained these applications and increased their work by sending all such applications for reports to the Directorate. The Secretariat felt that the large number of applications and complaints indicated the inefficiency of the Directorate which felt that this was an unnecessary interference from Government in examination work. The Secretariat was not able to indicate any cases where a complaint was justified. A work-study officer who examined many of these cases was also unable to find a single case of irregular condonation which contravened the principles of condonation used by the office. Why then so many complaints?

After a study, the work-study team discovered that the explanation to this mystery was to be found in the rules. The principles which the office had been following in granting condonations had *not* been incorporated in the rules which only stated that "condonations shall be decided by a committee of examiners".

In practice, the Department had adopted certain principles which were on the lines of the principles used for most examinations—*viz.* one grace mark for every percentage by which the candidate's total exceeds the minimum total required for passing. If for example, the minimum total for passing is 35 per cent, and a candidate scores 39 per cent in the aggregate, he is entitled to get 4 grace marks if he fails in a subject.

However, since these principles had not been incorporated in the rules it gave rise to two undesirable consequences:

(i) The candidates did not know the basis of condonation and therefore, ran to Government either for mercy or with complaints of favouritism, creating a problem of public relations.

(ii) It created a huge amount of work for the office which had to type statements showing the names and marks of all the candidates who had failed (nearly 5000) and put them before the Committee for condonation. Had these principles been a part of the rules, the condonations could have been decided by the office without the approval of the Committee which was a formality.

After some discussion, the office agreed to amend the rules.

4. Government offices are often afraid of or reluctant to amend Acts and rules. True, it takes some time to amend an Act or a rule; but a good dynamic officer should not be shy of it.

ANNEXURE 13-A

Office : The Director of Agriculture, Poona
Sub:—Supply of rain-gauge equipment to rain reporting centres.

Sr. No.	Date	From	To	Action
1.	14.3.61	Tehsildar (Officer i/c of the station.	Dir. of Agriculture	Requests for supply of a receiver and a measuring glass.
2.	23.3.61	Dir. of Agr.	Tehsildar	Sends two indent forms for being submitted through the Collr.
3.	....	Tehsildar	Collector	Submits indent.
4.	18.4.61	Collector	Dir. of Agr.	Submits indent forms duly countersigned
5.	2.5.61	Dir. of Agr.	National Instrument Fact. Calcutta	Sends the indent for supply of equipment direct to the station.
6.	17.5.61	N.I.Factory	Dir. of A	Quotes the price (Less than Rs. 50) and terms and requests for confirmation of order.
7.	7.6.61	Dir. of Agr.	N.I.Fact.	Intimates acceptance of prices etc.
8.	8.7.61	N.I.Factory	Dir. of Agr.	Sends a form for formal confirmation.
9.	25.11.61	Dir. of Agr.	N.I.Fact.	Reminds factory.
10.	27.12.61	N.I. Factory	Dir. of Agr.	States that the equipment duly packed was lying ready but could not be despatched as the nearest Rly. station was not known.
11.	4.1.62	Dir. of Agr.	Tehsildar	Asks him to intimate to the factory direct the nearest Rly. Stn.
12.	8.1.62	Tehsildar	N.I.Fact.	Intimates the name of Rly. Stn.
13.	5.3.62	N.I. Factory	Tehsildar	Despatches equipment

14.	10.3.62	N.I.Factory	Dir. of Agr.	Sends bill for payment
15.	15.3.62	Dir. of Agr.	Tehsildar	Requests for confirmation of receipt of equipment in good order.
16.	10.9.62	Tehsildar	Dir. of Agr.	Confirms receipt of goods.
17.	27.9.62	Dir. of Agr.		(1) Takes note in the Dead Stock Register (2) Asks the Accounts Deptt. to make payment.

ANNEXURE 13-B

Office : The Director of Agriculture, Poona,
Sub:— Supply of rain-gauge equipment to reporting centres.

There are 400 rain measuring centres in the State (i.e. nearly 15 per distt.) Each of these is in charge of some local official such as the Tehsildar or the Primary School Teacher. The equipment at each centre consisting of a small metal, cylinder, a collecting bottle, a funnel and two measuring glasses cost in all about Rs. 100. Parts of the equipment often require replacement and have to be purchased from the National Instrument Factory, Calcutta. The following case study illustrates the procedure followed for obtaining replacement:—

On 14.3.61 a Tehsildar in charge of a Rain Measuring Centre wrote to the Director of Agriculture who is in charge of all this work, for the supply of a measuring glass. On 29.3.61 the Director of Agriculture asked the Tehsildar to apply in the prescribed form through the Collector. On 4.4.61 the Tehsildar submitted the indent to the Collector who passed it on to the Director of Agriculture on 18.4.61.

On 2.5.61, the Director of Agri. wrote to the National Instrument Factory, Calcutta for the supply of the equipment. On 17.5.61 the factory wrote to the Director of Agriculture quoting the price for the equipment (about Rs. 40), the terms for the supply and asked for the confirmation of the order. On 7.6.61 the Director wrote to the N.I.F. accepting the price and terms. On 8.7.61 the factory sent the Director a form for formally confirming the order which he returned on 30th July, 1961.

As there was no further intimation from the factory, the Director reminded the factory on 25.11.61 and on 27.12.61 the Factory informed him that the equipment had been duly packed but could not be despatched as the nearest railway station was not known. So, on 4.1.62 the Director asked the Tehsildar to intimate to the N.I.F. direct the nearest Railway station which he did immediately on 8.1.62. On 5.3.62 N.I.F. despatched the equipment.

On 10.3.62 the N.I.F. sent the necessary bill to the Director who wrote to the Tehsildar to confirm the receipt of the equipment. On 10.9.62 the Tehsildar confirmed the receipt of the equipment and on 27.9.62 the Director took note in the Stock Regr. and asked the Accounts Department to make payment.

14

FORMS

Forms are an important means of work simplification in offices. They simplify work in two ways—

(i) By reducing writing work; and
(ii) By standardising the presentation of information, they facilitate the collation and processing of information.

2. There are two types of forms used in Government Offices—

(a) those to be filled by outsiders – *i.e.* members of the public and even by other offices; and
(b) those to be used internally by an office.

3. We are quite familiar with the forms in category (a) which everyone has to fill for railway booking or at Telegraph offices. We are also familiar with forms used for sending information to or receiving information from other offices but we often fail to make use of forms for several internal office operations such as for example—

(i) making leave applications and in sanctioning leave;
(ii) applying for and sanctioning loans from the Provident Fund or for house building or purchase of vehicles.

4. In these cases the applicant generally writes a lengthy application on which the office writes a note and then finally drafts a running memo or resolution granting or rejecting the application. It takes quite

some time for the dealing assistant to prepare for every case a new note and a new draft letter which are usually routine and repetitive and use some standard terms and phrases. The officer sanctioning the application has likewise to go through a new note and a new draft checking spellings, grammar, besides dates, amounts etc. which vary from case to case. All this can be avoided by the use of standard forms as can be seen from the example of a leave application shown in the annexures to this chapter.

Annexure -A : shows a leave application and the note and draft usually put up by offices. **Annexure-B** and **Annexure-C** show the same case dealt with with the help of forms.

5. One should note—

(i) the difference in the writing work involved in the two methods; and

(ii) the ease with which an officer can scrutinise the case with a form.

6. However, despite these advantages, offices are often reluctant to use forms for such routine work probably because writing a special note and draft order for a case gives the assistant a sense of doing some very important original work whereas filling a form appears to be just routine clerical work.

7. Such forms are however more useful only in large offices. In a very small office with just 8 or 10 workers, it may not be worthwhile getting the forms printed (or cyclostyled) and stored.

8. **Tenders, Contract-letters etc.:** Tenders or letters accepting tenders or quotations, often run into several pages of running matter mostly repetitive. Most of the matter in such letters or tenders is routine and repetitive except for details of goods, dates of supply, rates etc.; yet offices often type a fresh letter or tender form from A to Z for every case. In such cases, the non-repetitive portion such as — (a) description of goods; (b) prices; (c) dates of delivery; etc. should be separated from the main letter or tender form and included in a schedule or form at the end and the rest of the letter/tender/order can be got printed or cyclostyled. It then becomes a standard form though it looks like a letter or a routine printed order.

Care must, however, be taken to ensure that the main letter and the schedule are legally in order and signed by a competent officer.

Design of Forms

9. Whatever the type of form, the following principles or guidelines of design must be borne in mind in designing a form.

(1) A form has generally 5 parts—
   (a) Identification *i.e.* the name of the Department, its number if any, brief title:......etc.
   (b) Instructions for filling the form.
   (c) The main body of the form.
   (d) Concluding portion-signature of applicant, date etc.
   (e) The space for the receiving department to record its remarks, calculations, orders etc.

(2) The identification particulars such as the name of the Department, the number and title or the subject of the form should be printed in bold letters at the top of the form.

(3) The instructions should, as far as possible, precede the main body of the form. The practice of printing the instructions as an annexure at the end of the form is inconvenient for the person who fills the form. Quite often he notices these instructions after filling the form.

(4) The instructions should be short, crisp and direct. Avoid the passive voice. Here are two examples of how the instructions should be written:—

Wrong Way	**Right Way**
(i) The name should be written in full in block letters and beginning with the surname.	(i) Write the name *in full in block letters* beginning with the surname.
(ii) Salary certificate in duplicate from the employer should be attached to the form.	(ii) Attach *two* copies of the salary certificate from the employer.

(5) There should be adequate space for filling each entry. (In the current form for railway reservation used on the Central and Western Railways, the space for writing the train number is

about 3.5 cms while that for writing the name of the train which requires more space than the number, is only 1.5 cms.).

Here is a copy of the nomination form for elections used by an Institute.

Name and Address of the member in block letters	No. on the electoral roll

It allots just 6 cms. for writing the name and the address and 10 cms for the Roll number which does not require more than 2 cms.

(6) The spacing between two lines should be adequate.
(7) Application forms for licences etc. are often worded like letters as follows:—

> To,
> The Chief Officer,
> Timbactoo Municipality.
> Sir,
> I beg to apply for a licences for opening a hotel .... etc.
>
> Yours Faithfully,
> (XYZ)

All this is unnecessary.

(8) Avoid articles and unnecessary words.
(9) The entries in the main body of the form should be according to sequence e.g.

(1) Name of Bank (2) Branch (3) Account No. (4) Interest earned and not

(i) interest earned, (ii) Name of Bank, (iii) Branch (iv) Account No.

(10) The entries should be arranged to facilitate the tabulation mechanism in a typewriter as shown below:

Wrong Way

(i) Name of the applicant:—
(ii) Father's name:—
(iii) Name and address of the office where working:—
(iv) Post held in office:—
(v) Residential Address :—
(vi) Telephone Nos.:—
   (a) Office:—
   (b) Residence:—

Better Way

(i)	Name of applicant	:—
(ii)	Father's name	:—
(iii)	Name of Office	:—
(iv)	Post held	:—
(v)	Office Address	:—
(vi)	Residential Address	:—
(vii)	Telephone Nos.	:—
	(a) Office	:—
	(b) Residence	:—

This arrangement not only facilitates typing but also the scrutiny of the form and extraction of information.

(11) If the form is bilingual, instead of mixing up the entries in the two languages in a single form it is advisable:—

(a) either to print separate forms in the two languages; or
(b) to print it in one language on one side of paper and in the other on the reverse side (as the Railways have done for the Reservation forms).

(12) Forms especially those meant for the public should be printed on good clear *white* paper in bold print and should create a favourable impression on the person who has to fill it.

ANNEXURE 14- A

I. SPECIMEN LEAVE APPLICATION

Sir,

I have to go to my native place to repair my ancestral house before the monsoon. I, therefore, request you to grant me leave from 1st May 1984 to 20th May 84 with permission to prefix the holiday on 30th April and to suffix the holidays on Saturday and Sunday on 21st and 22nd May respectively. I shall positively resume on 23rd May, 1984.

I also request you to allow me to encash another 30 days of earned leave. As far as I have been able to ascertain, the total earned leave at my credit is 118 days.

Yours Faithfully,
X.Y.Z.

II. Office Note on Leave Application

Mr. X.Y.Z. Assistant in Section IV has submitted his application for leave for 20 days from 1/5/84 to 20/5/84 with permission to prefix the holiday on 30th April and suffix Saturday and Sunday on 21st and 22nd May 1984. He has also asked for permission to encash 30 days of earned leave.

According to the Accounts Section, Mr. X.Y.Z. has 117 days of earned leave (not 118 days as stated by him). So the leave and encashment is admissible.

The application has been submitted through the Section Officer of Section IV who has asked for a substitute; but as leave is for less than one month no substitute can be given especially as a large number of the staff is going on leave.

The following draft order is for approval

(Sd) P.Q.R.
Assistant.

(Sd) A.B.C.
Under Secretary Estt.

III. Draft Leave Order

Shri X.Y.Z. is granted leave from 1st May 1984 to 20th May 1984 with permission to prefix the holidays on 30th April and to suffix Saturday and Sunday on 21st and 22nd May 1984.

Sanction is also accorded to the encashment of 30 days of the earned leave at the credit of Shri X.Y.Z.

During the period of Shri X.Y.Z.'s leave, the Section should carry on the work by redistributing his work among the existing staff.

Under Secretary.

ANNEXURE 14- B

LEAVE APPLICATION

Deptt.:—

Date:—

1. Name of Applicant :—
2. Designation and Section :—
3. Nature of leave applied for:—

Type of Leave	from	To	Days	Leave at credit
(1)	(2)	(3)	(4)	(5)*
(a) Earned leave (b) Half pay leave (c) Half pay leave commuted (d) Extra Ordinary leave (e) Maternity leave				
* To be filled by the Accounts Section.				(sd) Head of Acctt. Sec.

4. Days to be prefixed :—
5. Days to be suffixed :—
6. Date of resumption of duty :—
7. Encashment, if any, required :—
8. Reason for leave :—

Signature of applicant.

---

9. Recommendation of Section Officer:—

Signature of Section Officer.

---

10. Recommendation of Office:—
11. Orders of sanctioning Officer:—

Signature.

ANNEXURE 14- C

LEAVE ORDER

Deptt.:—

Date :—

1. Name of Applicant:—
2. Designation and Section :—
3. Nature of leave sanctioned :—

Type of Leave	from	To	Days
(1)	(2)	(3)	(4)
(a) Earned leave (b) Half pay leave (c) Half pay leave commuted (d) Extra Ordinary leave. (e) Maternity leave.			

4. Days to be prefixed :—
5. Days to be suffixed :—
6. Date of resumption of duty :—
7. Encashment sanctioned :—
8. **Leave Arrangements:** (During the leave of Mr. X.Y.Z., Mr. P.Q.R. Senior Clerk in the Section should be promoted as Assistant).
9. **Posting after resumption :** Unless otherwise informed, on return from leave, Mr. X.Y.Z. should resume as Assistant in the same Section.

Sanctioning Officer

15

OFFICE MACHINES

Office machines play a useful part in increasing office efficiency and in reducing the drudgery of work. As compared to the developed countries in the west, we have very few types of machines used in offices in India and much less in Government offices. Before dealing with the few machines available in India, it is necessary to make a few general observations about machines.

2. The first is that with the limitations of resources, many offices especially in far off Tehsil places lack even the simplest office machine - the typewriter. On the other hand at higher levels like the Secretariat, there is a surfeit of machines which in most cases are under-utilised. They are often bought as fancy toys or status symbols. A few examples are given below:—

(i) A public undertaking in Maharashtra led by a really management oriented Chief Executive, bought tape-recorders (a novelty in those days) for officers who wanted to work on Sundays or holidays, so that there was no need for either the officers or their stenographers to attend the office on holidays. There were just 4 tape recorders for about 100 officers since not many officers worked on Sundays.
The news reached the Secretariat which then bought two tape-recorders for each Secretary — one to be kept in the office and one at the residence. In the public undertaking referred to above, even the Managing Director (who was an ex-officio Secretary) had just one tape recorder which he carried home and brought back to the office the next day. One doesn't know

how many officers in the secretariat ever used the tape-recorder for office work.

(ii) Today every senior officer has a photocopying machine (popularly called the xeroxing machine) which is not utilised even for one hour a day. Wouldn't it be more economical to keep just two or three common machines for a group of offices especially where offices are situated in an office complex?

(iii) Many senior officers are provided with personal computers. Most of them never use them or keep them with Personal Assistants who use them as sophisticated typewriters. If these computers are kept in the office and the rest of the staff is given adequate training, there will be better utilisation of the machines.

3. While Government offices are keen to buy new machines, they do not pay adequate attention to regular servicing or repairs and a large proportion of the machines lie unused.

4. With these general observations we shall now look to some useful machines. The pictures of some of the machines which are not in common use in government will be found in Annexure XV-A to this chapter.

(1) **Typewriters:** The most common machine one finds in the smallest and the lowliest office is a manual typewriter. Manual typewriters have been displaced by electronic typewriters or computers in most western countries and even in good commercial offices in India.

5. Electronic typewriters have several advantages over manual typewriters *viz.*:—

(i) The typing is very neat like printed matter;

(ii) There is sometimes a choice of different types and different sizes;

(iii) After typing each line, the typist can see the line on a small display screen, correct the mistakes, if any, and then print it on paper. The typed matter can, therefore, be absolutely spotless. In a manual typewriter once a wrong character is typed, it can be changed only by an eraser or by the use of a white correcting fluid. Apart from the time required for these operations, the output is usually not absolutely clean;

(iv) The neatness of a communication is further enhanced by perfectly straight margins on both the sides as in a book, by a mechanism by which the spacing between letters or words is automatically adjusted; and

(v) Most electronic typewriters have a "memory" in which you can store a letter. When the need for a similar letter arises in another case, we can "recall" the earlier draft, make the necessary changes and type out the second letter.

Inspite of these advantages of electronic typewriters, manual typewriters will continue to be used in India for at least 15-20 years because of—

(a) the price which is nearly half of that an electronic typewriter;
(b) the ribbons used for electronic typewriters are also costlier; and
(c) the lack of facilities for repairs and servicing in small towns.

In buying a typewriter one must also give some thought to the size of the roller. If the office has to type many statements, it is necessary to buy a typewriter of policy size or at least brief size.

(2) **Rotary duplicators:** These are popularly called cyclostyling (or Roneo) machines. (Actually Roneo is a brand name). These are of two varieties—manual and electrical. The rotary duplicator which makes copies with the help of a stencil is the cheapest method of making copies because of the comparatively low cost of the machine as well as the ink and paper used. (In fact very good quality paper like bond paper is unsuitable for rotary duplicators, as it does not absorb the ink quickly giving rise to smudging. This can, however, be prevented by rolling out copies slowly, allowing each copy sufficient time to dry. Even then, the appearance of copies taken out on rotary duplicators is not as neat and tidy as a copy taken out on a photocopier (or xeroxing machine. Xerox is also a brand name).

(3) **Electronic stencil-cutters (Fig. 4):** A major disadvantage of a rotary duplicator is that the matter to be duplicated has to be either typed on a stencil or etched with a pointed pen when one has to take out copies of a figure or a diagram. In the latter case the stencil often gets damaged. Further, it is impossible to duplicate pictures on a stencil. This handicap can be overcome by using an Electronic Stencil Cutter in which the matter (whether typed material or a picture or a diagram) automatically gets etched on the stencil by an electronic device. This electronic stencil cutter can etch even a picture with shadings, on a stencil. It also requires less time than typing a stencil and there is no need of proof correction.

However, with the advent of photo copiers, electronic stencil cutting has gone out of use.

(4) **Photocopiers or Xerox Machines:** Xeroxing eliminates all the problems of typing, copying pictures and diagrams and proof correction. It is a much quicker process and gives a very clean appearance if it is done on a good machine. Xeroxing, however, is a costlier process and cannot be used for duplicating on a large scale for which there are two alternatives.

(5) **Xerox Offset:** In the xerox offset process, the matter to be xeroxed, is transferred to an offset plate on an ordinary xerox machine and copies are then taken on an offset printing machine. This process is about 50 per cent cheaper than xeroxing; but it is not possible for every office to keep an offset printing machine even though table-top offset printing machines (costing about Rs. 3-4 lakhs) are now available. However, an offset machine or two can be kept in large office complexes like the Secretariat or at district headquarters.

(6) **Copy-printer:** For very fast and large volume of photo-copying work, we get copy printers which can give upto 100-120 copies per minute but the machine costs Rs. 4-5 lakhs as against about Rs. 1-1.5 lakhs for a xeroxing machine and unless the volume is very large, (say 1000 copies), the cost per copy is very high.

(7) **Fax (Fascimile) Machines:** Barely 5 years ago, a Fax (or fascimile machine) was a novelty. Today it has become as common as a xerox machine. A fax machine is a combination of a photo-copier (xerox machine) and a telephone so that a photocopy of a paper can be sent across on a telephone line. This is the fastest mode of transmitting communications. Besides, as in the case of a xerox machine, one can transmit diagrams, pictures and even *signatures.*

With the introduction of Fax machines, teleprinters are fast disappearing.

(8) **Franking Machines (Fig. 2) :** Next to the typewriter and the rotary duplicator, the franking machine is probably the oldest office machine available. It costs about Rs. 15,000 (manual) and Rs. 35,000 (electric). It is convenient in two respects—

(i) elimination of the messy work of moistening and sticking stamps;

(ii) simplifying the problem of safe custody and accounting of stamps. (There can be no pilferage of stamps).

However, franking machines are not very popular with Government offices for two reasons—

(1) The office has to take the machine periodically to a post-office and get it set for the amount paid. When the machine has printed stamps upto this amount, it stops working. This facility for setting machines is not available at all post offices.

(2) Franked letters cannot be put in a post box but have to be delivered at a specified post office.

(9) **Collator (Fig. 1):** This is a machine used to prepare sets of papers. Copies of each page are kept in a set of open drawers (called stations). On pressing a button, a sheet comes out from each station which can be collected and pinned. One cannot, however, collate more than 8 to 10 sheets at a time.

(10) **Binding Machines:** There are four ways of binding papers:—

(i) **Staplers:** Ordinary office staplers cannot staple more than ten to twelve pages. However, larger staplers can staple even upto 100-200 pages.

(ii) **Electronic Binders (Fig. 7):** The papers to be bound are put in a special type of plastic folder which has some binding material. The folder is placed in an electronic binding machine which, on pressing a button, binds the papers.

(iii) **Spiral** and **(iv) Comb binding (Fig. 9):** In comb and spiral binding the papers are punched at several places along the margin and are then bound together—

(a) by separate wires in comb binding; or
(b) by a single wire in spiral binding.

The binding wires are made either of metal or plastic material.

The binding looks very elegant and is often used for reports or projects presented to prestigious organisations; but is somewhat inconvenient if any pages are to be replaced.

(11) **Addressing Machines:** Government offices are often required to send circulars, resolution etcs. to a large number of addresses such as for example,

(i) to all Collectors, or Superintendents of Police; or
(ii) all municipalities in a state which may be more than 200;
(iii) all colleges or all secondary schools or some non-govt. organisations.

The usual method is to take a typed or cyclostyled list of all such addresses, cut out the name and address of each and paste it on an envelope. This is a time-consuming as well as messy method.

The work can be simplified by the use of metal plates for all addresses prepared with the help of addressing machines. Since these machines are being sold by the Bradma Addressing Machines Co., they are often known as Bradma machines.

There are two types of machines:—

(i) **Embossing machines (Fig. 10)** for embossing names and addresses on metal plates.

(ii) **Stamping machines (Figs. 8 & 11)** which are used for stamping names and addresses with the help of the embossed plates. (The metal plates are stacked in a column and on pressing a lever, stamps the name and address on an envelop and makes room for the next plate.

Unless an office has to make new plates frequently, it need not buy the embossing machine but can get these plates embossed from the company or from another office which has such a machine.

The stamping machine comes in two varieties—

(a) a small hand-operated machine which can be used if the number of addresses is modest — less than 500-1000.

(b) an electrical model which is necessary if the number of addresses is very large — (more than 1000).

(12) **Laminating Machines (Fig. 13):** It has been suggested in chapter 4 that important documents like agreements, maps, plans which are required to be preserved for a long period, or which are required to be handled frequently, should be laminated.

These machines are available in different sizes and types with *width* of 4 inches to 12 inches. There are also Roll laminators which can laminate continuously long sheets of paper.

(13) **Shredding Machines (Fig. 12):** Government offices have to be very careful about the disposal of old papers which are usually destroyed by burning. This is a wasteful and also environmentally harmful method. A better way is to use shredding machines which can shred each paper to small pieces and the shredded material can then be sold to manufactures of hand made paper or papier mache objects.

(14) **Computers:** Finally we come to the computer—the machine which, many people hope, will one day eliminate all paper work from offices. That day may be very far off for Government offices in India but one finds a sea-change in the attitude of Government offices to computers. At one time there was considerable apathy, indifference and in some cases downright hostility to computers but today one finds Government offices much more receptive to computers. The earlier apathy was because the large mainframe computers used about 15 to 20 years ago, installed in closed airconditioned rooms to which only a few operators had access, were an enigma to most people. The new Personal Computers (PCs) kept on an office table look like a combination of a typewriter and T.V. and can be touched and operated even by a clerical level assistant. The computerisation of Railway reservations has also helped to break down the prejudice against computers.

However, most Government employees still do not have an adequate idea of what a computer can do. Although a computer can be used for a variety of jobs such as drawing complicated designs, or operating a machine (as in a robot), its three simple common uses for administrative offices are—

(i) Word processing where it is used as a powerful electronic typewriter with a much larger memory.

(ii) For making large scale complicated calculations by the use of a "spread-sheet" which is a tabular form in which one fills some figures and then orders the computer to make the calculations as in the example given below:—

Name of employee	Basic Salary	D.A. at 70% of basic salary	H.R.A at 10% of basic salary	Total Emoluments	Deductions			Net Payable
					Income Tax	Pr. Fund	Total	
(1)	(2)	(3)	(4)	(5)	(6)	(7)	(8)	(9)
(1) Mr. A.B.C.	2050							
(2) Mr. D.E.F.	1950							
(3) Miss M.N.P	3340							

One just fills up columns (1) and (2) and the computer calculates and fills the other columns. This is of course a very simple example — but consider a table of 15-20 columns for a few hundred employees and imagine the time required to do the calculations even with a calculator.

The computer can do it in a few seconds.

(iii) The third use of the computer is storing any data and retrieving it. (This is done with a programme called Data-base). When you have to search for a book in a large library, by an author with a name like Smith or Joshi, you may have to thumb through fifty cards before you get the required card - if the book and the card are at all there. If you cannot find the card, at the first attempt, you may go over the cards again lest you have missed it in the first search. If, however, you put all the information about the books in your library on a computer, it can tell you in a few seconds whether the book is in the library or not. You can even find out if it has been issued to any member.

In chapter 3 it has been suggested that the office Inward Register can be computerised and Sectionwise print-outs of the letters sent to each Section can be used as pages of the Section register of cases. Further, if the Section registers can also be computerised, it becomes much easier to trace the movement of cases instead of going through dozens of cards or thumbing through several pages of a register. (The present writer had successfully introduced such a system in one small office of the Government of Maharashtra).

In all these cases, print outs of the data or calculations are available.

With the help of standard programme packages, the operations can be done even by an ordinary clerk, with some training.

For the computerisation of Section registers it is not necessary to provide each section with a separate computer. Two or more sections can share one computer with a separate terminal for each section. If the same computer is connected to a terminal with an officer (or his secretary) all movements of the case can be registered on one computer.

Offices have, however, to be careful about buying computers. Many offices are often taken for a ride by computer companies and buy computers not suitable for their requirements or very high capacity computers not required by them.

It is not proposed to go here into a detailed description of the various types of computers and how they work. One should, however, bear in mind four points:—

(i) Every Government should now have in the Administrative Reforms or O&M Division (or whatever other name it bears) a person well-versed in computers to advise Government offices on the purchase and use of computers.

(ii) Computers should be purchased only after such expert is satisfied about the need of the office and its ability to use it. They should not be bought as fancy toys or status symbols.

(iii) As suggested in the Chapter 19 on "Training", it is necessary to intensify computer training for Government offices.

(iv) In taking up a programme of computerisation, start with some simple operation in the office which creates confidence in computers.

Scanner and Modem : Computers were developed as super calculators but today are equally or perhaps more useful for storage and retrieval of information and for communication.

A small floppy disc of a computer can store the text of a few books while a *Compact Disc* can store all the pages of the Encyclopaedia Britannica. We find libraries especially professional libraries storing hundred of magazines and journals for future reference. All the important articles in such journals can be stored on a computer (without the necessity of typing them) with the help of a *Scanner*.

Likewise information stored on a computer can be transmitted over long distances with the help of *Modem*.

Can we eliminate files and store all the material in the files in a Government office on a computer? We can; but that will require a huge investment in computers. Further, it must be remembered that just as it is easy to store information in a computer, it is equally easy to lose information stored in a computer or tamper with it and so special precautions are necessary to safeguard the information. We cannot, however go into the details of this here.

ANNEXURE - XV-A

SOME USEFUL MACHINES AND APPLIANCES

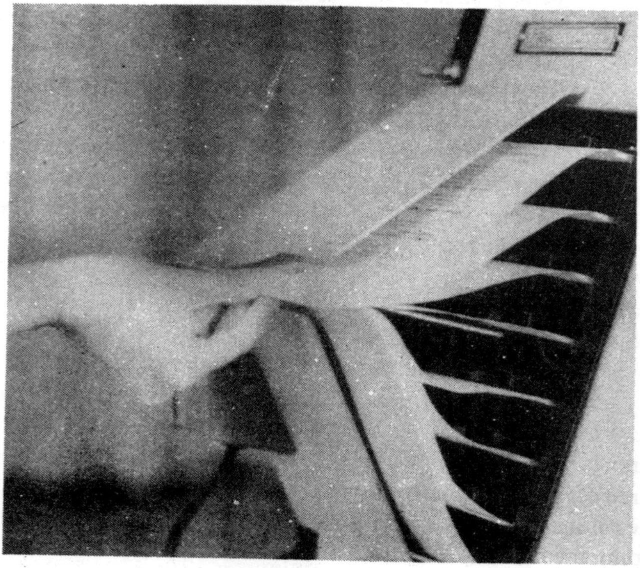

Fig. 1 : Collator

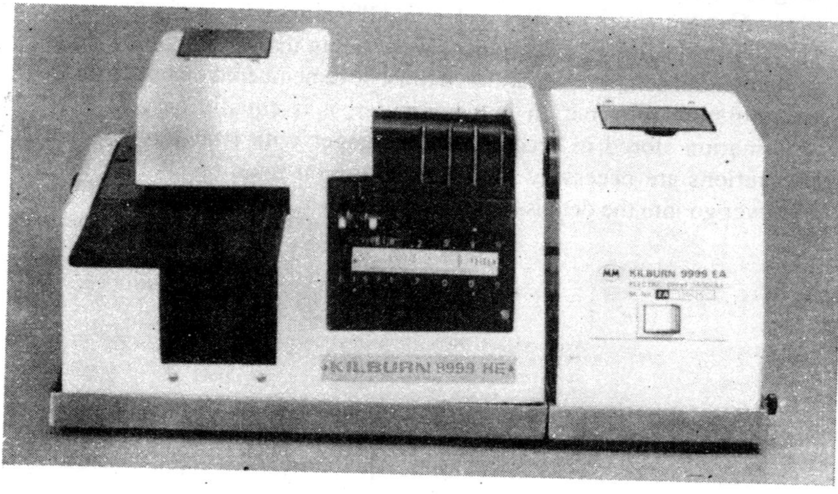

Fig. 2 : Franking Machine

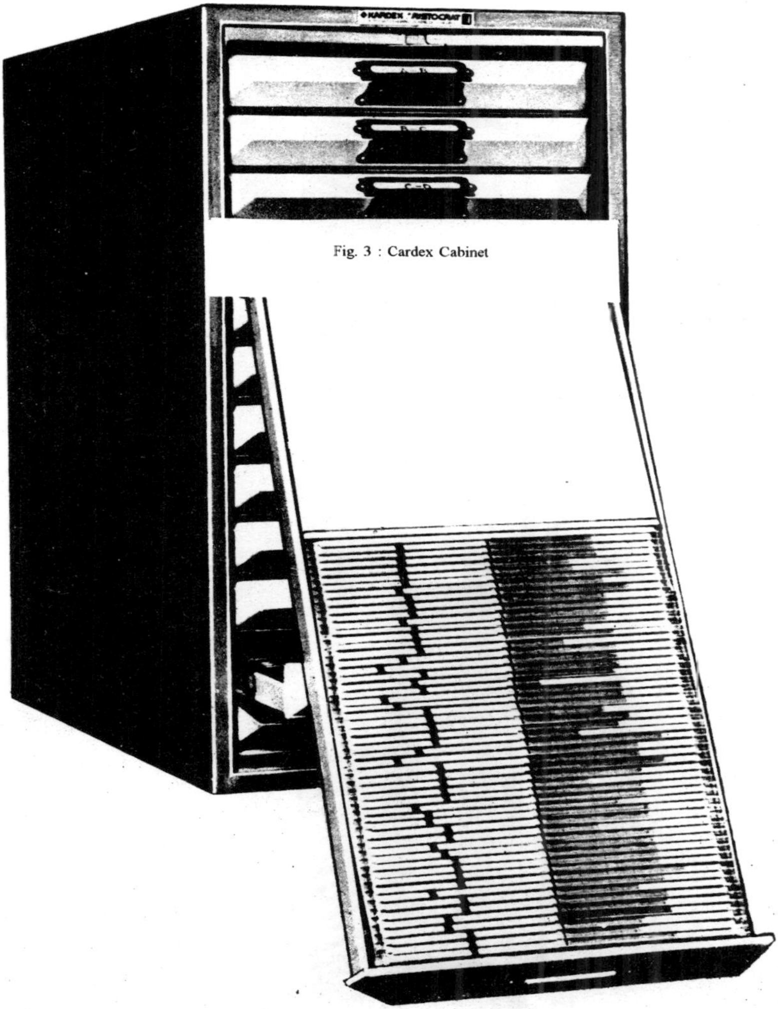

Fig. 3 : Cardex Cabinet

Fig. 3 . Cardex Cabinet

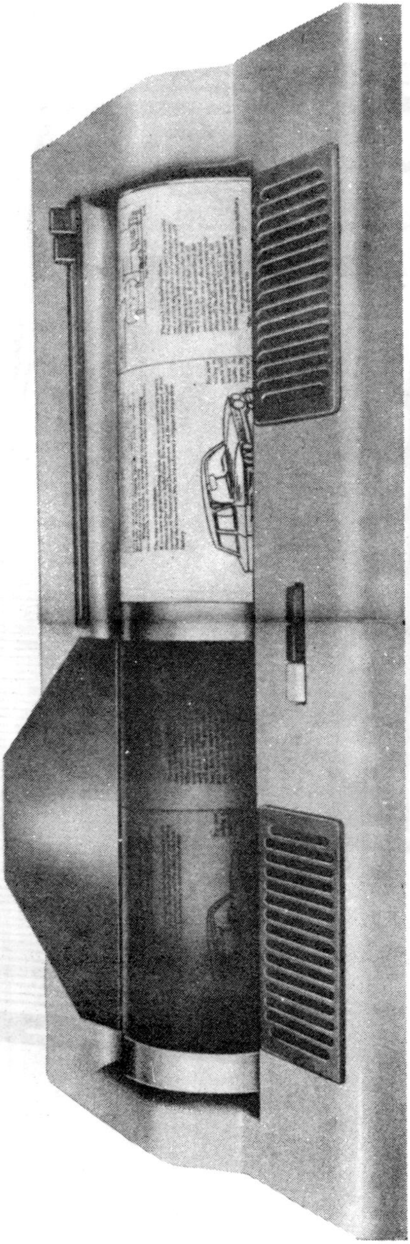

Fig. 4 : Electronic Stancil Culter

Fig. 5 : Table-top offset machine

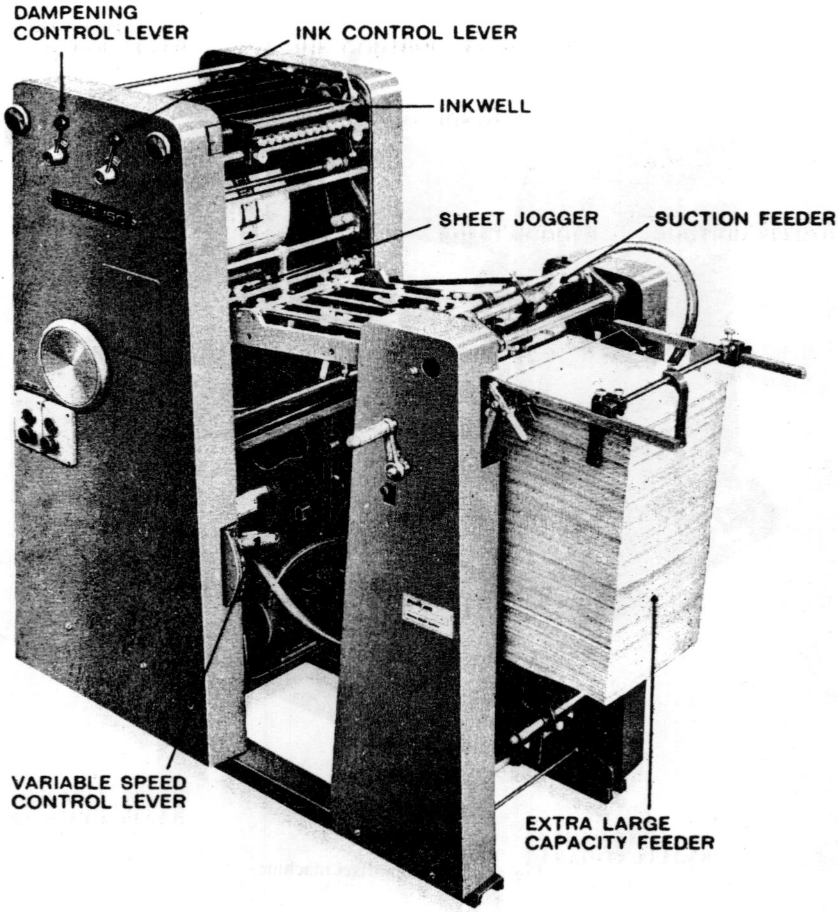

Fig. 6 : Offset Machine (large)

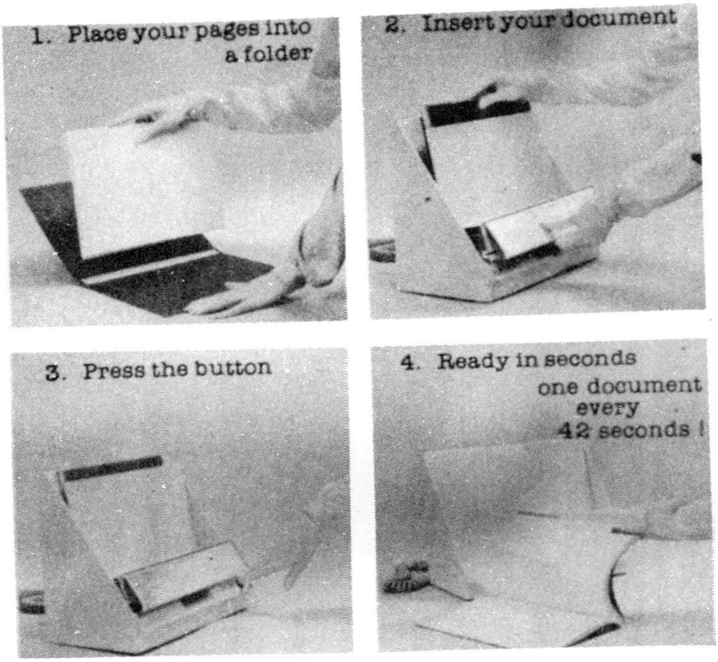

Fig. 7 : Electronic Binding Machine

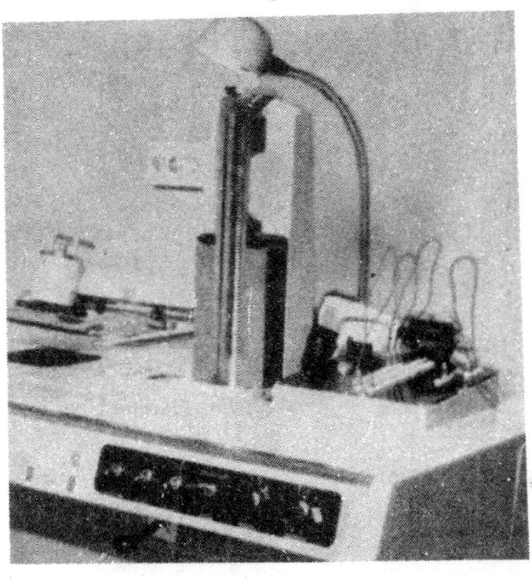

Fig. 8 : Addressing Machine (Electrical)

Fig. 9 : Spiral Binding Machines

Fig. 10 : Embassing Machine (for preparing address plates)

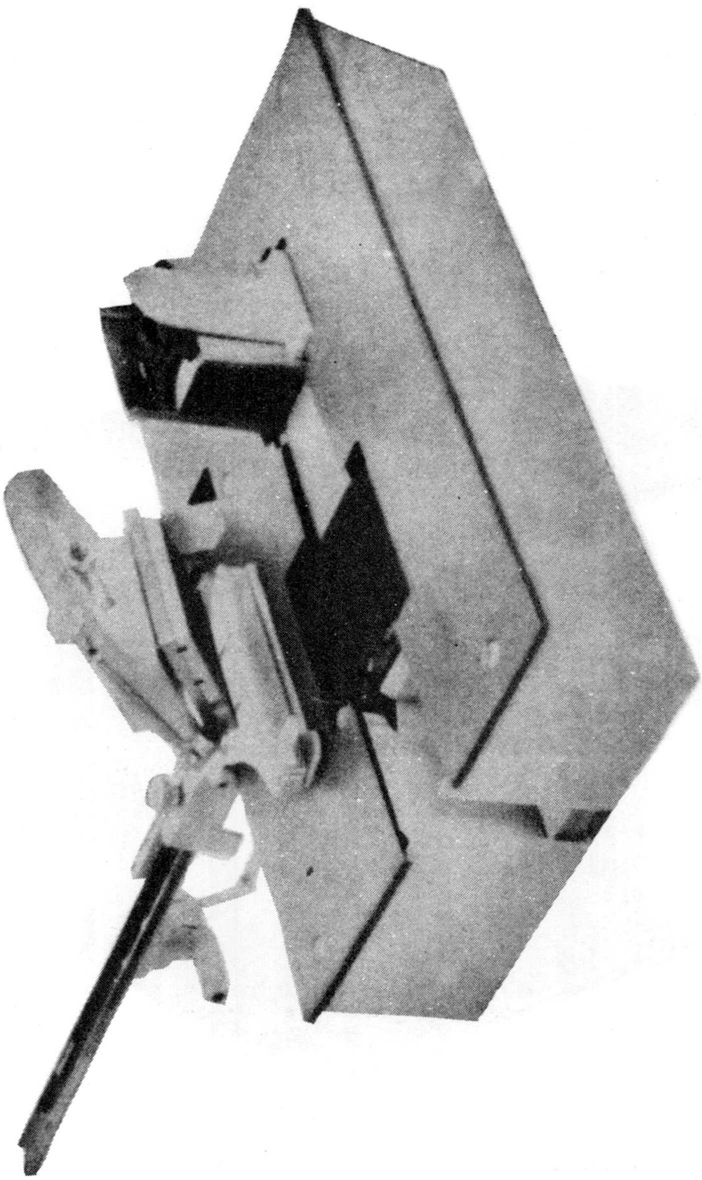

Fig. 11 : Addressing Machine (Hand Operated)

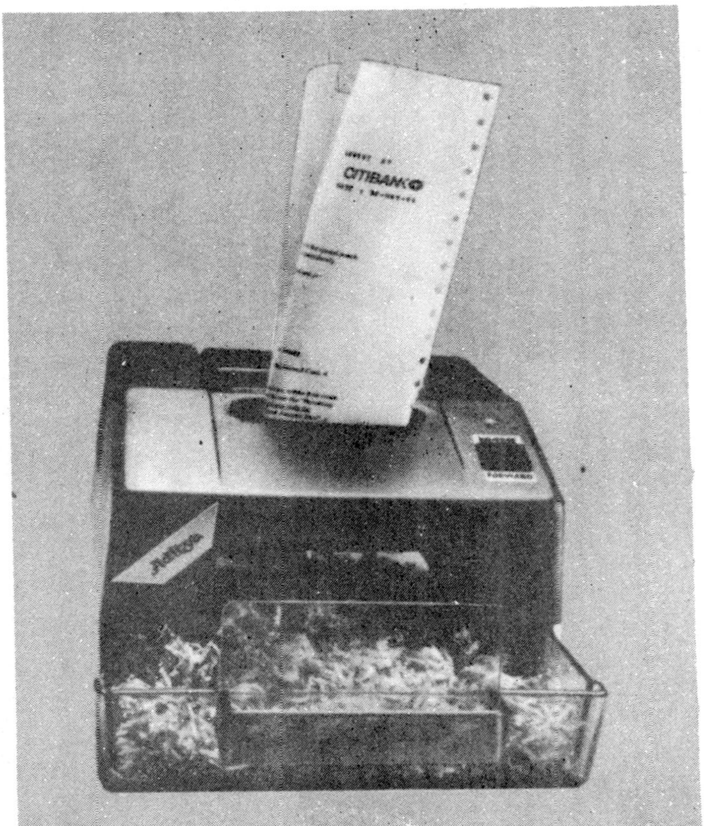

Fig. 12 : Shredding Machine

Fig. 13 : Laminating Machine (Large)

16

WORK MEASUREMENT AND STAFF ASSESSMENT

Kinglake has described the desert as "Sand, sand, sand, still sand and more sand, only sand and sand and sand again". Likewise Government offices always keep on asking for "staff, staff, staff, still staff and more staff, only staff and staff and staff again".

2. During the course of work studies whenever we asked an office what its problems were, the usual reply was "We need more staff". As one can see from the examples of methods -improvement in chapters 10 to 14, there are problems which cannot be solved by just sanctioning more staff. In fact, according to Parkinson, superfluous staff always creates more work to fill its surplus time. We often need changes in procedures, more delegation and in some case even changes in the organisational structure, rather than more staff which sometimes increases problems.

3. Offices often try to make a show of work by creating superfluous receipts. This is because of lack of any scientific approaches and methods of staff assessment in Government.

4. Whenever an office *feels* the need for additional staff (say about 5 clerks), it usually asks for 10 clerks, in anticipation of a cut from the superior office (usually the Finance Department). The Finance Department invariably rejects the proposal suggesting that the office is already over-staffed and can even cut down some of the existing staff. The office then comes back with some rigmarole about overwork, staff being inexperienced, the importance of its work and so on. This haggling goes on for months (sometimes years), before the Finance Department agrees to two or three clerks. Neither the Finance Department nor the office is satisfied. Both of them feel that they have been cheated.

5. All these *bazaar* methods can be avoided if we use some scientific or at least systematic methods to assess work and the staff requirement.

6. Work study provides for a number of techniques for work-measurement like—

- (i) Time and motion studies with the help of stop watches, micro-motion cameras etc.;
- (ii) Pre-determined time-motion standards; and
- (iii) Activity sampling.

These, however, are more useful on the factory floor where the workers do repetitive mechanical work. They can also be useful in offices to a limited extent in sections doing routine, mechanical or repetitive work like typing, despatching, making entries in registers, accepting cash or forms at counters....etc. They are not of much use for administrative offices where one Assistant does a variety of cases of varying complexity. For these we have to use some other methods of work-measurement and staff-assessment.

7. One must, however, note that before doing any work measurement or staff assessment, it is necessary to undertake a study of the methods or procedures. As the examples in Chapters 11 to 14 show, such a study can lead to either a total elimination of that particular item of work or reduce the work content by simplification of procedures. However, sometimes one has to go in for quick work measurement with the existing methods of work and without waiting for work simplification.

8. Subject to these caveats, we shall now see the methods of work measurement and staff assessment for Government Offices:—

(1) **Time and Motion Studies:** In this technique a Work-Study officer measures the time required for each item of work with the help of a stop-watch or even an ordinary watch. As stated above, this technique is useful only in routine and repetitive work such as—

- (i) entering a large number of vouchers in a register;
- (ii) accepting letters etc. at a counter;
- (iii) despatching letters;
- (iv) accepting cash and issuing receipts;
- (v) typing, cyclostyling etc.

There are some problems in the measurement of typing work because it involves a number of operations such as—

(a) inserting the paper in the typewriter (with carbon paper);
(b) adjusting margins;
(c) typing the number, date, subject, address etc.;
(d) typing the main matter; and
(e) typing the envelope.

In small letters of 3 or 4 lines a disproportionately large time is wasted in operations (a), (b) and (c); and so work-measurement of typing may be a little more complicated and time consuming. It can be done in the following way—

(i) Estimate the number of words a typist can type per minute or per hour;
(ii) Estimate separately the time required for items (a), (b), (c) and (e);
(iii) Estimate the number of words which can be typed in this time; and
(iv) Add this to the main typed matter in each letter.

In doing such work measurement, one has to take three precautions:—

(i) The workers selected for the work measurement exercise should be *average* workers—neither too efficient nor too inefficient. It is better to take two or three workers of average capacity.
(ii) In addition to the time allowed for regular tea and lunch breaks, one has also to make an allowance of 15% of the time for relaxation.
(After an hour of continuous work an office worker needs to relax for about 8-10 minutes (15% of the time).
(iii) One should not be too strict or parsimonious in fixing the time and give the impression of being heartless slave drivers. As far as possible, the work norms should be settled in consultation with the supervisors of the sections.

(2) **Predetermined Standards:** Most Government offices have some common items of routine work or practices such as—

(1) Making entries in the Inward Register of letters;
(2) Typing ;
(3) Despatching letters ;
(4) Preparing pay bills, travelling allowance bills;
(5) Orders about leave, Provident Fund, advances; and
(6) Mechanical work like sweeping offices and dusting furniture.

It is possible for a central organisations dealing with O&M or Systems studies or Administrative Reforms to make time and motion studies and lay down some common norms for all offices.

(3) **Activity Sampling :** Activity sampling is a statistical technique which is rarely used even in the private sector industries or offices because it is too sophisticated and time consuming. It can be used to find out answers to such questions as—

(i) How much time of an officer is spent on visitors, telephones etc?
(ii) How much time is a subordinate employee required to spend in discussing cases with an officer or in waiting outside an officer's cabin?
(iii) What is the proportion of time spent by the employees in an office in different activities such as — (a) working at the desk; (b) in discussing cases with officers; (c) in the canteen outside lunch hours; (d) in chit-chat etc.

The technique consists of visiting the place *unobtrusively* and making a note of what the employee concerned is doing or the number of employees in a room working at the desk or gossiping, or sitting in the canteen. As the quantum of such activities varies from day to day, depending upon the number of visitors or telephones that an officer receives or the number of calls that an employee receives from the officer, one cannot rely on the observations on one or two days but has to do the study over a long period and record a few hundred observations before drawing conclusions. This is, therefore, a time consuming technique but can be used occasionally on a limited scale.

To cite an actual example, during the work study of a hospital, the nurses complained about large absenteeism among ward-boys. When we checked with the muster, we found negligible absenteeism among the ward-boys for a whole month. So on some days selected at random, we checked attendance in a few wards and found about 20 per cent of the ward boys absent on each of those days. How could one explain the discrepancy ? Further discussion with the Administrative Officer revealed that the muster for the ward-boys was being maintained by a Chief Ward-boy who used to accept small bribes from the absent ward boys and mark them present. This Administrative Officer (a dignified Head Clerk) was unable to stop this mal-practice. So it was suggested that the muster for ward-boys should be kept in the office in charge of a senior clerk.

Two precautions are necessary in the use of this technique:—

(i) The number of observations should be sufficiently large — (at least a few hundred) and spread over a long period — unless the study is of a specific season — such as for example the Budget season or the Legislature session. Exceptional days when there is a large number of absentees because of dislocation of traffic or a strike, should be excluded.

(ii) The second precaution is that the time for making observations should be absolutely random. For example, if you visit an office regularly at 3.30 p.m. *every day,* you may find about 50-60 per cent of the clerks absent from their desks. Most of them are in the canteen for tea. Now if you conclude from this that the employees are away from their desks, about half the time, that would be an erroneous conclusion. The observations should, therefore, be taken at absolutely random times. This can be done with the help of Tippet's Random Numbers available in any good book on Statistics.

Measurement of Administrative Work

9. All the methods given above are useful for routine, repetitive mechanical work like writing registers, typing, despatching etc. or activities like answering telephone calls or going to the canteen. They are not of much use for administrative work. Some Government offices try to do work measurement (and staff assessment) by using some crude measure such as 10 "receipts" (letters etc.) per clerk/Assistant per day. Such attempts can be easily subverted by the offices by "creating" or "manufacturing" receipts by very ingenious devices such as (i) asking subordinate offices to send acknowledgement receipts of all important letters; (ii) taking out copies of trivial communications received by the office only for information and sending them to all sections in the office which treat them as new receipts; (iii) treating as receipts even handbills or advertisements received in the office. In one office which had developed

this into a very fine art of creating receipts, the present author found that nearly 20 per cent the receipts in the office were such bogus or manufactured receipts.

The following method used by us in work studies of Government offices was found useful. Administrative work can be divided into four categories:—

Category (I) : Absolute trash like copies of general circulars, copies of some communication issued by another office or section which are sent to all the offices or sections as a routine. They call for no action beyond a casual inspection and are straightaway filed after a cursory inspection.

Category (II): Simple cases like—

(i) Someone asking for a copy of an order or some simple information; and
(ii) Complaints on which reports have to be called for before taking any action.

Category (III): This category gives rise to most of the work in a Government office. These cases pertain to day-to-day problems that arise in Government. Some examples of such cases are:

(a) Personnel cases of appointments, promotions, leave, transfer etc.;
(b) Complaints in category (II) on which reports have been received from the field offices and the office has to examine how far the complaint is justified;
(c) Applications for grants, concessions etc. under rules or schemes;
(d) Sanctions for projects etc.;
(e) Legislature questions.

Category (IV): Very heavy cases involving—

(i) legislation, framing of rules;
(ii) a major project or scheme; and
(iii) a complaint case revealing some serious, lacuna, mistake or defect in the administrative machinery.

The Work Study Officer or O&M officer can analyse the work of each section for about a week or two by examining either the post (tapal) or the cases submitted to the officer — or by examining both, and prepare a table on the following lines—

Category	Average/week	Average time required per case	Total Time	
(1)	(2)	(3)	H	M
Category (I)	15	5 minutes	1	15
Category (II)	10	15 minutes	2	30
Category (III)	25	1 hour	25	00
Category (IV)	3 cases in week	—	10	00
			38	45

The estimates of average time required for each category of cases given in column 3 is only illustrative as it differs from office to office depending upon the nature of cases and the calibre of the staff. No estimate of average time can be given for cases in category (IV) because it can vary from some hours to days for a case regarding framing of some laws or rules or preparing a report.

10. The estimation has to be done by an experienced officer who should take into account—

(i) the time required for collecting previous papers or getting information from other sections;
(ii) the time required for typing, despatch etc. if these are done by the Assistant;
(iii) the calibre of an average Assistant; and
(iv) the time spent in discussing cases.

Precaution should be taken to consult the supervisor (Section Officer or Head Clerk) before arriving at an estimate.

Guinea Pig Technique

11. Quite often offices including supervisors refuse to accept the work-measurement done by a Work-study officer on the ground that with the quality of workers in his office, the norms suggested are too high. In such situations it is useful to try the "Guinea-pig" technique. A guinea pig is a small animal of the size of a mouse which is used for biological experiments. A human guinea-pig in work-measurement is a worker comparable to a worker in the office being studied who is used for work-

measurement. (During the work study of an office of the Maharashtra Government, which had asked for a hundred additional clerks etc., the Work-Study Officer found that the work load for the whole day prescribed for clerks in a certain section doing routine mechanical calculations, could be completed in 45 minutes. When the office started the usual excuse about the poor calibre of staff recruited from the Employment Exchanges, the Work-Study Officer called for a clerk recently recruited from the Employment Exchange from another office who completed the quota of work in just 50 minutes.

Change in Attitude

12. No scientific work measurement can be of much use unless offices and particularly higher level officers curb their craving for more and more staff. There was some justification for this attitude in the sixties and the seventies when, with the niggardly wage-policy of Government, the only way an honest Government employee could keep his head above the tide of inflation, was a small promotion which could be secured by expansion of staff. After the Fourth Pay Commission, the situation has changed radically particularly because of the linking of dearness allowance to the cost of living. True, one still cannot compare the salaries of Government employees with those in affluent companies in the Private Sector but today a Government servant with limited liabilities can at least live a decent life if not a life of luxury. Government servants should compare themselves, to passengers in a railway compartment which is already full but not crowded. Inviting more passengers into the compartment can only crowd the compartment and reduce their own space (or salary in a job).

13. In the case of higher officers, the lure is not only of money but of status. An Assistant Director wants to be a Deputy or Joint Director. So he manoeuvers and gets more posts of Deputy Directors—often superfluous posts. In the process, all the posts of Dy. Directors or Joint Directors are devalued in status. The respect which a Deputy Secretary could command in the fifties or the sixties, is not available even to a Secretary in many places today.

14. The third point to be borne in mind is that often many lower posts, particularly of clerks and peons (especially in mofussil offices) are created for the convenience of officers. I came across an office which had nearly 35 peons for a staff of less than 200 officers and clerks but was asking for more. When I pointed out to the Personnel Officer that they

had already too many peons, he gave me the following deployment of peons:—

	No. of peons
1 Director	- 6 (2 in office
	(2 at home (called bungalow peons)
	(1 working as driver
	(1 working as gardener
1 Joint Director	- 4 (2 in office
	(1 bungalow peon
	(1 driver
5 Deputy Directors	- 10 (1 in office
	(1 bungalow peon
8-10 Asstt. Directors (Class II)	- 5 (often taken out on tour).
Casual absentees	-3-4 every day.

That left hardly 6-7 peons for office work which included despatch, carrying papers within office ...etc. I was speechless.

15. The institution of "bungalow" peons was justified at a time when there were very few telephones at the residences of officers. Although "bungalow" peons have been abolished in many Governments, senior officers still insist on having such peons who are usually used for domestic work.

Casual Leave

16. Casual leave, especially among the lower staff, is another factor which reduces the out-put of Government offices. Most developed countries do not have this system; but in India (and probably in most of the under-developed countries) it is a part of the office culture even in the Private Sector. Apart from reducing out put, it also disturbs the office schedules of work which is very annoying. An officer plans to do some work on a particular day but finds that the concerned clerk is absent. One office of a Public Sector undertaking in Maharashtra led by a Management oriented Managing Director, reduced this nuisance by providing for the encashment of unenjoyed casual leave (as in the case of earned leave). However, he also earmarked one peon to attend to personal chores of all the staff—such as payment of bills, renewal of licences, ration cards etc. As against a quota of 10 days of casual leave per annum, the average casual leave enjoyment in this organisation was about 3 days in a year.

This system is worth a trial in other Government offices.

17

CONTROLS

1. The Management process consists of four steps as shown in the diagram below.

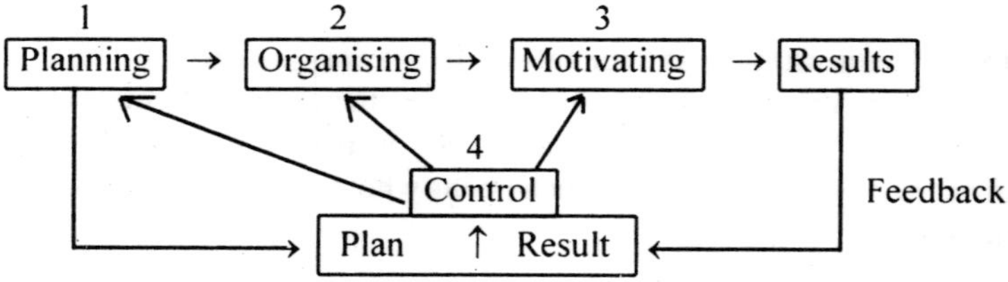

They are—

(1) Planning — a project, a scheme or any work with a time frame for its execution;

(2) Organising — which includes setting up an organisation, and procuring men, machines, materials and money;

(3) Motivating — inducing the people to carry out the work willingly; and

(4) Control — to check whether the work is progressing according to plan.

2. The process, however, does not end with control. If control indicates that the work is not progressing according to plan, we have to make changes in the plan or the organisation or the methods of motivation.

So, for effective control, one must have a plan against which performance can be checked.

3. For the purposes of control, work in a Government Office can be divided into 4 categories—

Category I : Work which is to be completed by a certain time-limit. This includes construction of buildings and installation of machinery, starting a new institution or a new activity in an existing institution, organising elections, conferences or similar programmes or even getting some urgent laws, rules and orders passed by a certain time limit.

Category II: Watching the progress of expenditure against budget grants or the collections of revenue against budget estimates.

Category III: Other administrative work mostly arising from correspondence relating to schemes, complaints against lower offices, preparation of various bills and making payments in time — which continues to flow through the office throughout the year. There are usually no time limits for most of such work but it is necessary to ensure that it is done within reasonable time.

Category IV: Routine housekeeping checks in office such as ensuring the maintenance of various registers like the cash register, Provident Fund registers, stationery and dead-stock registers and checking them from time to time.

4. Different techniques and methods are necessary for these four categories of work; but before we consider these methods it should be emphasized that control has to be exercised basically by the *person who performs or manages the work* with periodical checks by his superior officer or office.

Methods and Techniques

5. **Category I:** For work in Category I, especially for very complicated works like building projects which require the co-ordination of a number of activities and agencies, one can use techniques like PERT/CPM. But these are very sophisticated techniques and need a person specially trained and experienced in their use. They can be used for large projects where one can appoint at least a part-time person with special training and experience in the use of these techniques. One finds that even most of the engineers in Government are not sufficiently familiar with this technique. We shall not, therefore, go into the details of this technique which the reader can find in any book on Management.

6. Much more useful for Government offices is the technique of "Bar-charts" also called "Gantt charts", named after the person who

invented them. Annexure 17-A to this chapter shows a bar-chart for purchasing and installing a machine. The reader can see that this technique can be understood and practised even by a clerk in a Government office who has not studied beyond the school-level. For comparison Annexure 17-B shows the CPM chart for the same work.

7. It should be noted that these techniques (PERT/CPM and Bar-charts) which were first devised for engineering works can be used even for administrative work like holding elections or arranging large conferences which require the co-ordination and completion of several activities according to a schedule.

8. **Category II:** For work in this category, periodical reports prepared and submitted to a superior office or officer are very useful. There are two types of reports — one to be submitted to a superior office or officer and the other to be received by the office. One can see that in the Ahmednager Experiment (see Appendix18-A) the files relating to these periodical reports were required to be kept in a separate 'bundle'. In many offices two charts listing such reports were displayed on the wall behind the Section Officer (like the charts hanging from a patient's cot in a hospital). This practice has now been discontinued in most offices.

9. A common deficiency about such periodical reports (such as the expenditure against budget grants or tax collection against the budget estimates), is that there are usually no pre-determined control figures to compare the actual performance with. These reports are filed after a cursory inspection and it is only after the receipt of eight or nine monthly revised estimates that the office wakes up to the slow or fast progress of expenditure or tax collection. It is, therefore, necessary to lay down some control figures or targets for all such items, in consultation with the officer concerned at the beginning of the year.

10. **Category III:** Work in this category which is usually called "administrative or correspondence work" constitutes the bulk of work in an office. It comprises a variety of cases including approval of schemes and projects, complaints from the public, cases referred by lower offices for orders, and house keeping work like sanctioning appointments, leave, transfers, payment of various bills ... etc.

11. Most of this work emanates from communications received in the office which have to be "disposed of". The disposal may be of three types—

(a) It may require some simple action like sending the letter to another office for disposal and filing the papers;

(b) It may require action which may take months and sometimes even years, as for example,—

(i) if it requires a report from a lower officer who in turn has to make some enquiries from his field offices;
(ii) if it requires the office to frame some legislation or scheme or project;
(iii) if it is dependent on some question under consideration in the same office or, in another office or, in a court;

(c) On cases in category (b) above, the office receives a number of communications like reminders from the parties, ad interim reports from other offices, enquiries from superior offices which require some simple action such as attaching the communication to the original file and taking awaiting orders from the superiors, or giving some ad interim reply, or issuing a reminder to some other office to whom the original letter may have been sent for enquiry.

12. Whatever the type of communication and its disposal, it is necessary to see that the clerk or assistant takes the required action without much delay. Delays on the part of office workers (even in forwarding applications to other offices for a report) are an important cause of corruption at low levels. A system requiring each dealing Assistant to maintain *a work sheet* showing the number of each communication received by him, the subject and the date on which action was taken by him, is useful.

13. Every section in the office should then be required to submit an Arrears Report every week after giving the assistants or clerks reasonable time to deal with the communications. In large offices, a consolidated Arrears Report should be submitted to the Head of the office.

14. Two precautions are necessary to make such Arrears Reports effective. First, as pointed out in para 2, there should be a control-figure or parameter. In pre-Independence days in the Bombay Secretariat the Sections were given one week to take action on letters received during the previous week. Therefore, at the end of the second week the staff was expected to dispose of all the communications received during the previous week and show *zero* arrears. The control figure was, therefore, *'0'*. (Of course everyone realised that this was only an ideal (or a target) which could not be realised for want of papers, or the fact that there were some

heavy cases which could not be disposed of within a week; and so arrears of about 5-10 communications per Assistant out of about 40-50 communications received during the week (or about 20-30 arrears per section), was considered good performance.

15. One day a senior officer in charge of the O&M Division in the Secretariat 'discovered' that this method of preparing the Arrears Report was not correct; and communications reported as "pending up to 1 week" were actually pending for *more* than one week. So an order was issued that instead of submitting the Arrears List at the end of the second week, it should be prepared at the end of the week in which the letters were received so that letters etc. reported to be pending "upto 1 week" were *in fact* pending upto 1 week. When it was pointed out to the O&M Division that it was not possible to dispose of all the letters received during the week by the end of the week—especially the communications received during the last 2-3 days, they said "We do not mind if all such cases received during the last 2 or 3 days remain in arrears. We do not worry about the number of letters in arrears "upto one week".

16. The Arrears Report became more "accurate"; but in the bargain there were two undesirable consequences—

(i) The control figure of zero arrears under the previous system was lost. The cavalier approach - "We do not worry about he figures of arrears upto one week" meant that there was no control figure; and

(ii) Sections started showing large numbers of arrears "upto one week". Gradually the "upto one week" arrears went into "upto two weeks" and still later "upto three weeks" and so on. Very soon the arrears went out of control.

17. One Department ignoring the orders of the O&M Division adopted a via-media of allowing the office 2 working days after the end of the week, to enable the office staff to dispose of at least most of the simpler cases received during the week and submitted the arrears report not on the last day of the week (*i.e.* Saturday) to which the list pertained, but on the Wednesday of the following week. The result was the restoration of the control figure to *zero* and a much better control on arrears.

Periodical Census of Pending Cases

18. As explained in para 11 above, there are cases which take months or

sometimes years to come to a close. Think for example of an application for evacuee property on which a report may have to be called for from our High Commissioner in Pakistan or a case which is held up because one of the parties has approached a court.

19. Howsoever prompt or efficient an office may be, it just cannot make progress in such cases. There are, however, many such long-term cases which remain pending ("in await" is the official term) because of sheer lethargy or indifference of the office. The case may have been kept pending for general orders of Government on all such cases, which may already have been received in some other section. The present author as a Deputy Secretary had come across several cases for the extension of municipal limits and establishment of new municipalities because of an impending census. (No changes in municipal boundaries are allowed for a specified period before and after a census.) The cases had however, been kept in await for several years after the census ban was over.

20. It is, therefore, useful to have a periodical review of such cases once in 3 or 6 months. For this purposes (like banks closing their normal work on 31st December and 31st July), Government offices should stop all regular work on a specified day once every 3 or 6 months and review all pending cases.

21. In the erstwhile Bombay State there used to be such reviews in which the Under Secretaries were required to examine personally all the cases in their sections pending for more than 6 months. This practice now seems to have been discontinued.

22. **Category IV:** These are essentially internal controls in an office and have to be checked periodically by the superior of the person who is supposed to maintain these registers and occasionally even by the head of the office. A check of these registers is an important aspect of the inspection of every office by a superior office.

Inspections

23. Inspections form an important method of control and supervision of all aspects of office work. Usually there are prescribed norms for inspections. These include—

(a) the periodicity of inspections, and

(b) the items to be checked during such inspections for which it is useful to have standard check-lists.

24. There are two categories of inspection—

    (i) inspections of a lower office by an officer or a team from a *superior* office; and
    (ii) internal inspections by an officer *within* the office.

Offices are usually quite enthusiastic about inspections of the first type (*viz.* inspections of lower offices) because these give the staff of the superior office an opportunity for a little outing and a break from the daily routine. However, officers are usually reluctant to carry out the second type of inspections within the office because—

   (i) It means additional work without any compensation;
   (ii) It is somewhat awkward, especially for officers promoted from the office, to check the work of people with whom they have to work all the time. (Some of them might have even been their colleagues at lower level only a few months earlier); and
   (iii) Deficiencies in the work of one's own office or section can be a reflection of one's own slack supervision.

25. The author has seen Under Secretaries in the Maharashtra Secretariat sitting down with their Section Officers and filling up routine inspection forms without even stepping into the sections. Therefore, inspections should not be left only to the immediate superior, but there should always be multi-tiered inspections. If an Under Secretary is required to inspect his Sections once in a month, a Deputy or Joint Secretary above him should also be required to inspect the sections at least once in 3 or 4 months and the Secretary should inspect at least a section or two in a year.

26. Inspections are always more effective if they are carried out as surprise inspections. However, an officer carrying out such surprise inspections must be human enough to understand that in such a surprise inspection he cannot expect the office or section to be in a perfectly spic and span order and should high-light only such deficiencies or defects as are of a very serious nature. For example, if the cash-book has not been tallied for three or four days, it can be ignored except for a mild oral warning, but if the cash-book shows a large deficiency in the cash, that cannot be ignored.

27. Inspections, especially audit inspections, are usually an exercise in fault-finding. It is time the inspecting and audit officers adopted a more positive and helpful approach and tried to find out what the difficulties of

the office are, sort them out if possible and make constructive suggestions for the improvement of the office. The difference between a traditional or audit-oriented inspection and a work study oriented inspection can be best understood in the following way.

A traditional Inspector asks, "Why is this register incomplete?"

A Work Study Officer asks—

(1) Is this register necessary ? [See the O&M Approach in chapter 10]

(2) If yes, why is it incomplete? What are your difficulties in the maintenance of this register? How can you improve this register and its maintenance?

28. In pre-Independence days some states like the U.P. (then called United Provinces) had a separate Inspectorate for offices which used to carry out inspections of all offices in a professional way. This was abolished in the thirties as a measure of economy. It is worthwhile setting up such Inspectorates again and to give their work, O&M or Management orientation. When O&M was introduced in Government offices in the fifties, it was combined with inspections. Unfortunately as explained in Chapter 20, activities like O&M and Work Study have almost been discontinued in most Governments.

Finally, one must remember the old dictum, *what is not inspected is usually not done.*

Pursue Files and Parsurams

29. The Head of every organisation or office is technically responsible for all the types of controls referred to above. However, in the case of very large offices or organisations, it is impossible for him to control every aspect of office work and has necessarily to leave many of these routine controls to lower officers and keep a selective watch on a few items. For example, he may not be able to keep a watch on the arrears of all the sections but he may have to keep a special watch on the arrears in some important section or a section in which arrears are abnormally high.

30. An erstwhile Chief Secretary of Maharashtra had devised a very ingenious system of watching such critical problems. Whenever he became aware of such a problem he would dictate a small two line note on the following lines—

(1) "What is the latest stage about the drafting of the bill for a new Rent Act ?".

(2) "Have we received the Report of Messers XYZ on the Mandovi Bridge collapse?"

(3) "What is the latest position about arrears in the Lands Section?"

31. One copy of the note was sent to the concerned officer and the second copy was kept in a file by his Staff Officer or P.A. Every week or fortnight, the P.A. or the Staff Officer would go to each of the officers and ask him to record below the note, the latest position about the problem. The file with the latest reports from the officers was submitted to the Chief Secretary every week or fortnight.

32. He used to call the file "Pursue File" and so the Staff Officer got the nickname "Pursuram".

A Warning

33. No human being usually likes controls and so inspections are usually disliked by all lower officers and offices. One must, therefore, be careful not to introduce over-control or erratic controls. I give below three examples of such over and erratic controls.

(1) One over-enthusiastic Secretary who had come into the IAS after a stint in the Private Sector was very enthusiastic about controls and Management Information Systems and prescribed a large number of periodical reports for the District Medical Officers (called Civil Surgeons). These included a *daily* report about family planning operations not only at the District Hospital but at all the public and private hospitals in the district. Imagine the work involved in collecting such information every day. Some of the District Medical Officers whom the writer met at a training programme, complained that they had stopped doing medical work and had become Head Clerks preparing and submitting statements. After a few months the officer realised the futility of such statements and reduced their frequency.

(2) An ICS Officer in the fifties known for strict but often senseless discipline, insisted that every letter or case coming to the office should be disposed of within 2 days. (The officer

> was also fond of fining people even for small delays and mistakes). Now, there are cases in Government offices, especially those at higher level, which just cannot be dealt with in two days—or even in two months. For example, if you are dealing with some proposals for a new legislation, you have to study similar legislation on the subject in other states or even other countries and you may need some weeks to study the problem. All such arguments were useless before the officer.

The result of this rigid rule was that the office workers somehow managed to push files from their tables with some pointless queries or references to other offices. Worse still one officer in one Collectorate told the present writer that in complicated cases with many enclosures, the clerks sometimes used to destroy copies of minor documents and ask the applicant to send copies. Till these copies arrived, they would get some time to examine the case at their own pace.

(3) These however were whims or idiosyncraries of individual officers. Much more harmful is interference with established systems of the office.

In paragraphs 12-21, I have explained how the Bombay Secretariat used to control arrears with - (1) weekly arrears reports, and (ii) a periodical review of pending cases. After the reorganisation of the states in 1956, the system of periodical review fell gradually into disuse but a fairly good control on arrears was maintained through the weekly arrears lists prepared by each Assistant and Section Officer.

In 1975, along with a Desk Officer system several other changes were also introduced and one of these, was the abolition of worksheets for Assistants and the system of weekly arrears reports based on these worksheets. Instead, a section-wise list of pending cases (not letters) was submitted to the officers. Obviously there could be no control figure and it was difficult to asses the state of work by counting the pending "cases" because, as stated earlier, Government offices are full of cases pending for months and even years-primarily because of the nature of the cases.

To give an analogy from our private lives, the weekly arrears lists were like a monthly income and expenditure account. The cases which are not yet finally, disposed of are like the assets and liabilities which we have accumulated over the years. The first thing that a prudent person worries about is his monthly income-expenditure account and then he checks his assets and liabilities like the bank balance, the investments and the outstanding loans etc. at intervals of a few months. If he ignores his monthly income-expenditure account and looks only to his bank-balance he will probably soon be bankrupt.

After one or two years, Government realised the importance of the Assistants' work sheets and reintroduced the weekly arrears list but by that time sufficient damage had been to the system which has still not been restored to its former efficiency and reliability.

ANNEXURE - 17-A

GANTT (OR BAR) CHART FOR THE PURCHASE AND INSTALLATION OF A MACHINE

Activity ....

Waiting period ....

		May				June				July				August				Sept.				Oct.			
Activity	Week	I	II	III	IV	I	II	III	IV	I	II	III	IV	I	II	III	IV	I	II	III	IV	I	II	III	IV
1. Appoint Experts' Committee and call meeting		1																							
2. Committee meets to identify suppliers; write to suppliers for quotation				2																					
3. Receive quotations - tabulate and call meeting of experts								3																	
4. Selection of suppliers – Issue letter of intent to supplier									4																
5. Prepare agreement, consult Legal Adviser, send it to supplier										5															
6. Receive signed agreement													6												
7. Pre-installation fittings																						7			
8. Receipt and Installation of machine																							8		
9. Decide staff and advertise														9											
10. Receive applns., short-list and call for interview																		10							
11. Interview, select and issue letters of apptt.																					11				
12. Staff joins																							12		
13. Train staff and inaugurate																								13	

ANNEXURE - 17-B

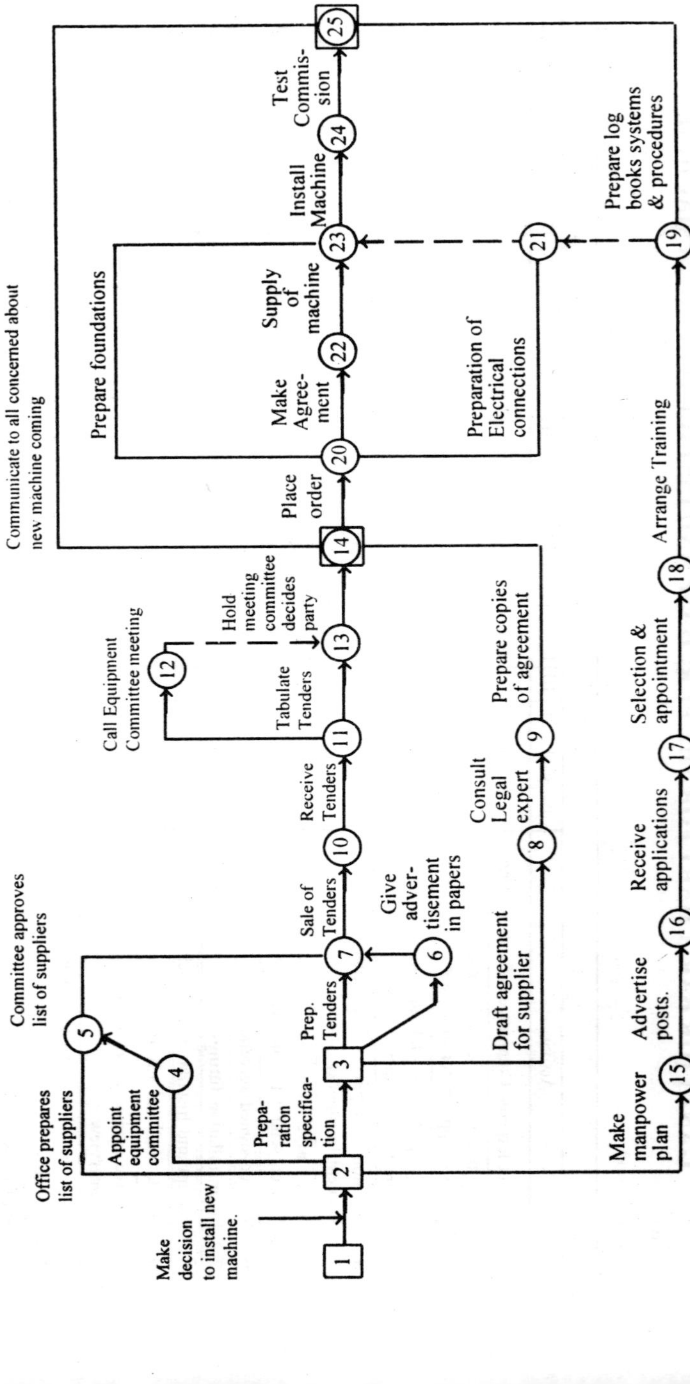

NETWORK FOR PURCHASE AND INSTALLATION OF MACHINE

18

SUPERVISION IN OFFICE

Hitherto we have dealt with the mechanical aspects of work — the maintenance of records, efficient systems of retrieval, the structure of the office organisation, improving the efficiency of methods of work....etc.

2. While these are all essential for the efficiency of an office, they are often rendered ineffective by the lack of motivation on the part of the office workers. Even Fedrick Taylor the father of Scientific Management was aware of the importance of motivation but believed that motivation depended upon the satisfaction of the material needs of the workers which could be achieved by paying more wages for extracting more work.

3. As stated in Chapter 1, the Hawthorne experiment using Taylor's own approach, if not exact methods, proved the importance of non-monetary or non-material factors and in particular the role of the supervisor in office efficiency.

4. It is not possible to go into the details of the various theories of motivation here but it is necessary to note three things—

(1) Initially the Hawthorne experiment gave rise to the Human Relations theory which led to a number of misleading ideas of being goody goody to the workers, mixing with them, patting them on the back and in general to adopt a soft approach. Later studies and theories recognised that the cultivation of good relations alone was not enough but the principal object was to get work done.

(2) In certain organisations and certain situations one may have to use even old fashioned harsh methods to get the work done — as for example when you are fighting on a battle front or in a crisis like a fire or flood or earthquake.

Today, therefore, the Human Relations Theory has given way to the Human Resources approach which regards human beings as one of the resources along with others like materials, machines and money. The theory, therefore, emphasizes making the best (or the optimum) use of such human resources by whatever method is the most suitable in the given circumstances.

(3) Whatever theory or approach you follow, the *supervisor* has a crucial role in the successful working of an organisation.

Who is a Supervisor ?

5. In a way, every officer in a Government organisation from the Cabinet or Chief Secretary down to the last Head Clerk in a tehsil office is a supervisor but the term supervisor is usually used for the lowest level person in an office supervising and getting work done from office workers like assistants or clerks who do only their own work and who are not responsible for the work of any other workers. Intermediate level officers like Deputy or Under Secretaries or Deputy or Assistant Directors get the work done through the first line supervisors like Section Officers, Superintendents or Head Clerks. Therefore —

Intermediate level Officer	—	decides what work should be done and lays down time limits and other para-meters.
First-line Supervisor	—	gets it done;
Worker (*i.e.* Asstt. or clerk)	—	actually performs the work.

6. In Government offices even senior level officers like Secretaries and Joint Secretaries are often required to deal with very important cases themselves and not leave them to clerks or assistants; but these are exceptional cases. The bulk of the work in Government offices is got done by the first line Supervisors from their assistants and clerks.

7. However, a Supervisor (at any level) should never over burden himself with original work but should always leave himself enough time for his other functions (see the following paragraph) which are more important. In particular, he should always have some time to think and to plan. Fredrick Taylor the father of Scientific Management used to say, "Managers must think".

(One of the undesirable features of the Desk Officer system introduced in Maharashtra in 1975 was that it expected the Desk Officer (the first line supervisor) to do most of the original work leaving him very little time for other important duties like training of assistants or inspection of his Desk).

Functions of a Supervisor

8. These include:

(i) Distribution of work among his assistants;
(ii) Laying down time limits for urgent or special cases (other cases are supposed to be disposed of within a reasonable time and in any case before the submission of the next arrears list;
(iii) Guiding assistants in difficult cases and providing assistance in specially heavy or difficult cases. An assistant may also need assistance in getting information from another office or another section in the same office;
(iv) Training assistants. In training workers, the Supervisor must not just prepare his own clones or stereo-types but should encourage assistants to develop new ideas;
(v) Inspect from time to time, the tables of his assistants and the various registers etc. required to be maintained in the section. [See that the section library, if any, is in order];
(vi) Maintain a diary or calendar showing the dates by which some important cases or returns are required to be submitted or received;
(vii) Maintain harmony among his assistants by resolving their *inter se* disputes in a fair manner;
(viii) Help the assistants as far as possible, in dealing with their personal problems with the office. (An assistant staying very far or with ailing parents may need some concession in attending office). However, as far as possible he should not get involved too much in personal problems of his subordinates; and
(ix) Make a *fair* appraisal of the work of each assistant especially at the time of the annual Performance Appraisal Report (called the Annual Confidential Report in Government).

Annual Confidential Reports

9. This is an important part of the Supervisor's function which unfortunately is not being done adequately in many offices at present.

10. The Performance Appraisal report in a commercial office is looked upon as an instrument for the development of the employee which ultimately benefits the organisation. If an employee has some deficiencies or defects, remedial measures such as training or transfer to a suitable post are considered. In Government organisations before Independence, the annual confidential report was looked upon as an instrument of punishment or revenge against employees who are either incompetent or shirkers or against whom the superior officer has some grudge. This was further helped by the form and method of assessment which in most organisations are trait-based or based on personality characteristics rather than performance based. The reports are, therefore, usually very subjective.

11. To make the reports (at least somewhat) objective, supervisors are asked to keep "Ephemeral Rolls" in which they are expected to note both good and bad incidents but very few supervisors do this and the reports are, therefore, based on general impressions, the personal relationship with the assistant (which in India is often clouded by caste and communal considerations) and some significant incidents (called critical incidents in Management literature) during the last few months before the writing of the Report.

12. But a greater problem in the writing of Confidential Reports today is the reluctance of Supervisors to write anything adverse against any assistant in the Confidential Reports. Every assistant is certified to be "very intelligent", "very hard-working" and "deserving accelerated promotion". This 'softness' in office supervisors is a post-Independence development which in many cases reduces the report to a ritual or a farce. It also does injustice to good workers.

13. Reforms in the system of these Reports would be beyond the scope of this book.

Qualities of a Supervisor

14. The qualities required of a supervisor differ from job to job and from situation to situation. A supervisor who is very efficient at desk work is sometimes unable to speak in a meeting or make arrangements for a small function in the office; but broadly an office supervisor needs the following:

(1) **Knowledge :** He must have thorough knowledge of his subject–not only knowledge acquired from his files or office manuals but he should go out and collect additional

information relating to his subject in other countries or other states. He should maintain his own files of such additional information besides having up-to-date information in respect of his own organisation.

He should also have sufficient general knowledge of what is happening in the world or his own country or state.

(2) **Technical Skills:** The technical skills of an office supervisor include ability to note and draft and the interpretation of legal instruments like Acts, rules and regulations.

(3) **Interpersonal Skills:** These are necessary to deal with—

- (i) his own staff with whom he has to interact all the time;
- (ii) his superiors; he is the link between his superiors and his assistants;
- (iii) his peers i.e. other supervisors and members of the office staff; and
- (iv) members of the public who may come to see him.

Inter-personal skills include ability—

- (a) to talk fluently and communicate your view point;
- (b) to listen to the other person patiently and sympathetically. (Government officers often have visitors with all kinds of grievances and problems (even domestic ones) for which they expect the Government to find a solution. They also make some impossible demands such as getting them accommodation or admission to a school or ask the Police to arrange for a special protection for his house ...... While turning down all such requests, one has to keep a cool head and give the visitor the impression that inspite of all your sympathy, you are powerless to do much for him. It is advisable to underplay your powers, if any.

(4) **Conceptual Skills:** These give you the ability to think of any problem from a broader angle and a higher plane and to see the inter relationship of all the parts of a problem. As you go higher up, you need this conceptual ability more and more than routine knowledge and technical skills.

Types of Supervisors

15. As supervisors are human beings, they cannot all be of one uniform type. They differ considerably because of their personal abilities, their social and family backgrounds and their experiences in life. Basically, however, they fall into two categories:

(i) Work oriented *i.e.* more concerned with getting the work done; and
(ii) Employee oriented *i.e.* more concerned with maintaining good relations with their assistants than getting the work done.

The ideal supervisor is one who can achieve both these goals with a fair degree of success.

16. From the point of view of attitude to employees, supervisors fall into four categories:

(i) **Autocratic** — who impose their own decisions on their assistants without giving them a chance to express their opinions. Such supervisors are usually ruthless with their assistants.
(ii) **Benevolent Autocratic** —who are basically autocratic so far as their decisions are concerned but are kind and generous to the employees in personal matters.
(iii) **Participative** —who listen to and respect the views of their subordinates, accepting their suggestions if they are reasonable.
(iv) **Laissez faire** —who are happy-go-lucky people who are not worried either about their work or their assistants and allow the assistants to do what they like.

17. Studies have shown that in general the worst type of supervisor is the *laissez faire* one while the best is the participative type. Organisations led by autocratic supervisors sometimes give better results so long as the leader is on the scene; but if for any reason he disappears, the organisation becomes rudderless and crumbles. On the other hand, organisations led by participative leaders can carry on the work efficiently and effectively even if the leader is absent. If the leader leaves the organisation permanently, someone from the team usually comes forward to take his place.

18. The practice of many supervisors of not taking their assistants into confidence is very harmful for the organisation. The case of the World

Bank Mission cited in Chapter 3, is also a case of failure to take one's assistants into confidence.

19. In another case a Secretary to a State Government put up some proposals to the Cabinet without consulting the office or even his Deputy Secretary. After the Cabinet approved the proposal, it was noticed that the proposal was contrary to certain basic financial rules and conventions of Government. Participative management in Government, therefore, is *not just desirable but essential.*

A list of 'Do's and 'Don'ts for Supervisors

20. It is not easy to change one's attitude and style of working very easily; but the list of 'Do's and 'Don'ts in Annexure 18-A at the end of this Chapter can help a supervisor to examine his methods of supervision from time to time and improve his approach and methods. It can also be useful to superior officers in assessing the work of supervisors in their organisation.

ANNEXURE - 18-A

SOME 'DO'S AND 'DON'TS FOR SUPERVISORS

Work

(1) If all the assistants complain about over work, check the work load of your section with that of others.

(2) If only some of the assistants complain about over work, check if there is fair distribution of work among the assistants.

(3) If an assistant experiences sudden pressure of work due to increase in work in his subjects, or some domestic problems, try to give him some relief by redistributing work.

(4) Encourage your assistants to take interest in each other's work.

(5) When an assistant comes to you with a complaint (often an unjustified one) listen to him patiently and then take your decision.

(6) If an assistant annoys you by some act like remaining absent or being late on a crucial occasion, do not rush into making a complaint. There may be some very sound reason beyond his control - such as breakdown of transport, or serious illness at home.

(7) If an assistant comes to you with a problem at work, try to help him. (Employees in Government offices often have complaints like inability to get stationery or a peon for despatching a letter).

(8) Make sure, however, that the employee does not get into the habit of running to you for every small problem. Teach him to find solutions for his problems.

(9) If an assistant makes a *bona fide* mistake, try to protect him as far as possible. If the mistake is because of his obstinacy or persistent carelessness, do not hesitate to punish him *provided* you have warned him about it before.

(10) In any case never berate or scold your assistants in the presence of strangers or other assistants.

(11) If you are pleased about a particular piece of good work done by an assistant, communicate your appreciation to him.

(12) If you have a particularly bright or better educated assistant under you, do not look upon him as a rival and run him down but look upon him as a disciple to be developed, unless he tries to be too big for his shoes or tries to run you down.

(13) Do not be too harsh or too lenient to the assistants in writing the annual confidential reports.

(14) Always keep notes in a diary about any exceptionally good piece of work or an exceptionally bad mistake made by an assistant.

(15) If there is some new scheme or new type of work, consult all your subordinates and get their opinion. You need not accept their advice.

(16) Try to cultivate team spirit by a monthly get together or a yearly excursion; but it is not advisable for very senior officers like Secretaries, Directors etc, to be too familiar with subordinates. Familiarity often breeds contempt; second, it is difficult to enforce discipline in the case of assistants with whom you are too familiar. In particular, it is not advisable for such senior officers to join the clubs or associations of very junior employees.

(17) Do not try to probe into the family life of an assistant. If, however he himself comes to you with some problem, try to help him without getting involved too deeply. In particular avoid any monetary dealings with your assistants.

19

TRAINING

Training is an important mode of improving efficiency but has not yet been given sufficient attention in most civil Government Offices. In many private sector organisations the training needs of an employee are required to be indicated in the annual Performance Appraisal Report. In the Defence Forces, officers are required to attend some training courses and pass examinations before every promotion; but as the Administrative Reforms Commissions pointed out in its report, the expenditure on training in civil administration is just about 0.5 per cent of the salary bill. The Commission recommended raising it to 1.00 per cent.

2. Except in some specialised departments like the Defence forces, the Police and the Fire-Brigade, there were hardly any training institutions for Government employees before Independence. No one thought of any training for office-workers who were mostly trained "on the job" by their superiors. This was adequate for an era when work was limited and did not change much in nature or volume over years. Civil servants including officers did not usually get promotion to the next higher post for about eight to ten years and had all the time in the world to learn on the job.

3. After Independence there were two significant changes:

(i) The nature and the volume of work started undergoing very rapid changes. There were frequent changes in Government policies, programmes, and in legal instruments like Acts, rules, and regulations.

(ii) The offices also expanded very rapidly giving rise to quick promotions for civil servants who were also required to man new departments. (The rate of expansion has now somewhat slowed down).

4. It is, therefore, no longer possible to depend only on "on-the-job" training. Most Governments have, therefore, set up training institutions for officers but there are very few institutions for the training of office staff most of which is non-gazetted (Class III or Group III as it is called today). Even the facilities for the training of officers except certain special categories like the All-India services, the Police service, the Forest service or certain technical services, are not adequate as can be seen from the following example from Maharashtra.

5. According to a census of Government employees carried out in Maharashtra in 1985, there were about 26,000 officers, and about 3,64,000 lower level staff (non-gazetted staff as they are called). A general training institution at Pune provides training for about 2000-2500 officers in a year. It will, therefore, take at least 10 to 12 years to put all existing officers through at least one training course; and there are new officers being recruited or promoted every year. The training capacity is thus not sufficient even for officers who constitute barely 6-7 per cent of the total staff (excluding Class or Group IV employees).

6. There are no training institutions for the Group III staff but many offices do arrange some lectures for employees appearing for departmental examinations — usually delivered by some of their own officers not all of whom are fit to teach.

7. During the present writer's long experience as a visiting lecturer at training institutions, he came across several such class III employees who had just been promoted as officers but who had never attended any training course in twenty or twenty-five years of service. On the other hand, this was the group most keen on learning new things.

8. It is impossible to arrange institutional training for such a large number of non-gazetted employees spread all over a State or the country in the case of Govt. of India offices; nor is it desirable to leave them entirely to "on-the-job" training or amateurish training by their own officers. The following experiment is, therefore, worth a trial.

9. Training is usually of four types—

(a) Various rules, like the Civil Service Rules, Discipline Rules, Budgeting principles and rules, Contingent expenditure rules .... etc. common to all departments;

(b) Some simple principles and techniques of office management including instructions in noting, drafting and communication;

(c) Attitudinal training for supervisory personnel; and

(d) Special Acts, rules, regulations, manuals and policies administered by each department.

10. For items (a), (b) and (c) above, which are common to all departments, Government can appoint some itinerant or peripatetic regional or district trainers who like the "barefoot" doctors of China can visit the offices of all the departments by turn and hold training classes (preferably part-time or out of office hours so that there is not much disturbance in the work of the office).

For the special subjects administered by each department, the department can appoint some of its own officers who can likewise visit all the offices of the department by turn.

11. Such barefoot trainers need not be full-time Government employees but can be retired officers who can be paid a fee per training session.

12. Such a scheme can provide some training for lakhs of non-gazetted office workers at a fraction of the cost of training at an institution. Some rough calculations made by the present writer indicate that the cost of training at a central institution (excluding the travelling and daily allowance paid to the trainees and the capital cost of setting up the institution) can eome to about Rs. 800-1000 per trainee, per day whereas the cost under the "in-house" scheme outlined above, will come to hardly Rs. 20-25 per employee, per day.

Institutional Training

13. Apart from inadequacy of training facilities, there are a few other problems about institutional training.

(1) Trainees are usually selected in an ad hoc manner. The person sent for training is either a blue-eyed boy of the establishment who is sent for training as a reward for good work; or an employee with a poor record who can be spared easily without affecting office work. The latter type of trainee usually lacks the urge to learn and looks upon his training as a holiday at Government expense.

During his long association with Government training institutions, the writer found that about—

(a) 25-30 per cent of the trainees are genuinely interested in the training;
(b) about 40-50 per cent have only casual interest; while
(c) 20-30 per cent totally lack any interest and are often a distraction for the class.

(2) There is no test for or evaluation of trainees at the end of most training programmes which is one of the reasons for the lack-a-daisical attitude of the majority of trainees.

(3) The few trainees who have picked up some new knowledge, skills or techniques at the training institution, often find it difficult to make use of them because, on their completion of training they are transferred to some new job which has no relation to the training received. This is particularly the case with senior officers going for long duration courses. Even an officer returning to his old job, finds it difficult to implement any new ideas or knowledge, because of the apathy (often hostility) of other colleagues who haven't had the benefit of such training, and in many cases even of his supervisors.

(4) There are two types of batches at training institutions

(i) homogeneous batches of officers from one department, and
(ii) mixed batches of officers from several departments.

Under the first pattern, a sizeable number of officers from a department or office get training simultaneously which can make some impact on the office. Under the second pattern, just one or two officers from an office receiving training, cannot make much impact on the office and as explained earlier, often find it difficult to put their training to use.

However, heterogeneous batches are more suitable for attitudinal training courses or special courses in common subjects like Public Relations, Planning, Budgeting etc. where officers from different backgrounds can make useful contributions from their varied experiences.

Training in Computers

14. One area in which training needs to be expanded and intensified is computers. The advent of table-top Personal Computers (PCs) has completely revolutionised office-work in the Western countries and even in

some of the more advanced commercial offices in our country. They are now even thinking of paper-less offices. That is a far cry for our Government offices where computers are still regarded with curiosity, fear or indifference. This is due to two reasons—

(i) the lack of sufficient access to computers especially for people at lower levels; and

(ii) prejudice born out of ignorance at almost all levels.

15.With the present Personal Computers, user-friendly languages and standard programme packages, even a clerk can work on a computer without undergoing a long course in computer programming.

16. The present writer who has arranged quite a few introductory courses (of just 2 or 3 days) for supervisors and middle-level officers like Deputy or Under Secretaries, found that most of them did not know what a computer could do and were surprised to find the speed with which a computer worked and the ease with which it could be operated even by a person who had never seen a computer before. Most of these officers however complained after the programme that they had forgotten all that they had learned in the two or three days for want of facilities to practise on a computer again.

17. Therefore, a one-time training course of even ten to fifteen days in a state level institution is not enough but it is necessary to arrange in all important towns where computers are being used by Government offices, computer classes where, besides full-time courses of two or three weeks, Government employees should be allowed to practise on a computer for at least one hour every day on the payment of a nominal fee. This would be like practice classes in short-hand or typewriting or post-literacy classes in literacy programmes.

18. The present writer was also instrumental in introducing a computerised follow-up system for a small but important office. The office was relieved of all the drudgery of filling up registers, scanning them for outstanding replies and then issuing handwritten reminders. The system worked very well for about three to four years and was then given up. Why? Because the clerk who had been trained in computer operation was transferred on promotion and the office did not have another trained man. A computer (with programmes) bought for about Rs.1 lakh was lying idle on a side rack.

20

ADMINISTRATIVE REFORMS

Government (or any large organisation like a University or a Municipal Corporation) is like a huge machine turning out various products and services. So long as it produces a limited number of products in small quantities without much change in either the number, the variety or the volume of products, it does not require much attention beyond normal maintenance with occasional replacement of some worn-out parts. We often do come across such machines which have been giving good service even after a hundred years.

2. However, if such a machine is required to change its products or their volume every few years, it requires much more than routine maintenance. It may need additional units, new processes and even new marketing methods.

3. In pre-Independence days Government was a simple but solid machine doing only law and order work with a bit of welfare work by way of free primary education or a few free hospitals and dispensaries. It did not bother itself much about social problems like untouchability, dowry, widow remarriage or economic problems like poverty, unemployment or uneven distribution of wealth except when such problems impinged on law and order. Under these conditions, it did not require many drastic changes. Occasionally the Government machinery was reviewed by a committee or commission at intervals of about 20 to 25 years. The reports of these committees were read more for their sonorous language than for their recommendations which were usually very mild and marginal and yet took years of further discussion and debate before they were implemented,—if at all.

4. This was however, a good approach because too many, rapid or

radical changes often cause more damage than good to an organisation.

5. This situation, however, changed radically after Independence. The old law and order state took on additional activities of welfare and development and had to be reorganised and changed more frequently to meet its ever-changing new responsibilities.

6. Initially for a few years after Independence, the method of committees and commissions to suggest improvements in the structure and methods of administration was tried but this was too slow a method to keep pace with the rapid changes in the functions of Government and so, from 1950 onwards, Government started experimenting with some modern Management techniques—called Organisation and Methods (O&M) or Work Study — and later on System studies.

7. In 1954, the Government of India established an O&M Division in the Cabinet Secretariat and small O&M units in other Ministries. Similar units on a smaller scale were also set up in many States. However, most of the people working in these units did not have any training in the application of these techniques and sometimes not even the aptitude for such work. They just did some routine work like monitoring arrears, the progress of legislature questions or important letters. Their pet remedies were prescribing registers and returns which only increased the work of offices. O&M became a bye-word of ridicule.

8. Round about 1960, mainly because of the efforts of two officers of the Special Reorganisations Unit (SRU) of the Finance Ministry, regular work study units with trained officers were started in the Government of India and many of the State Governments. Their work was much more useful than the earlier O&M units. In 1965, the Government of India established a full-fledged Administrative Reforms Department. However, in most of the States these work study units started declining primarily because of poor direction and apathy of senior administrators. In some States they are given routine work like monitoring arrears, legislature questions, dead stock registers, letters from V.I.Ps and in one state even promoting the regional language in administration. Although these are important functions, they are essentially maintenance functions and do not contribute to the improvement or reform of administration. It would be useful to set up in every State Government, a well staffed and well trained organisation to carry out administrative reforms continuously. (The Government of India already has a full-fledged Department of Administrative Reforms).

9. The chart below gives a broad outline for such an organisation for administrative reforms.

The organisation should have—

(i) At the top, an Administrative Reforms Council as explained in para 13 below.

(ii) A head of the rank of an Additional or Joint Secretary well-trained in modern Management who should be the Secretary of the Administrative Reforms Council.

(iii) Below him there should be a Work Study Division with 3 or 4 work study or systems study teams each consisting of an Under/Assistant Secretary and one or two Assistants.

(iv) An Inspection and Monitoring Division with 3 or 4 Inspection Units each consisting of an Under/Assistant Secretary and clerks to do *Management — oriented* inspections as suggested in Chapter 17 on Controls. These inspections should be in addition to the routine inspections carried out by the Departments dealing with the respective subject.

(v) An Environment Division with an engineer and supporting staff to study office lay-outs, furniture, adequacy of space and amenities like water supply, lunch rooms etc. (As the Ahmednager Experiment showed, this is important from the point of view of motivation).

(vi) A Computer Division to help offices in computerising work.

10. The number of study or inspection teams or staff suggested above is only illustrative. The actual numbers would depend upon the volume of work. Precaution must, however, be taken to see that only trained persons with aptitude for such work are appointed for the work. The decline and decay in the Administration Reforms Organisations in most states was due to the neglect of the quality and training of the staff.

11. The pattern of working should be on the following lines:—

Step I: The Inspection Division should carry out a preliminary inspection and indicate the problems and problem areas of an office or department. It should also inspect the routine maintenance functions.

Step II: A Work Study team should then study in detail these problems including the organisation of the office or department and its procedures.

Step III: The Computer Division and the Office Environment Division should study the problems of computerisation and office lay-out, furniture etc., if the Work Study or Inspection Units indicate the need for such studies.

12. In many State Governments these Administrative Reforms Organisations are under or part of the General Administration Department or the Personnel Department and, therefore, usually ineffective. The organisation can be more effective if it is placed under the Finance Ministry /Department) in Government because the ultimate object of these reforms is to deliver good service at minimum cost; and in Government, except the Finance Department, no other Department is interested in economy. As stated in Chapter 16 on work measurement, Government departments are normally interested only in expanding their empires.

Administrative Reforms Commission /Council

13. We have said earlier that in the context of rapid changes in the nature and volume of work, the old tools of administrative reforms *viz.* committees and commissions are not adequate; but that does not mean that they have become obsolete or useless. Work studies or systems studies are somewhat low level reforms in the day-to-day work. There are much broader questions such as creation of more All India Services, privatisation or reduction in the number or public sector undertakings, decentralising Accounts and Audit work, improving relations between politicians and civil servants....etc. Most of these are controversial questions of policy far beyond the scope of work or systems studies and we do need high level committees or commissions to consider them. However, because of the rapid pace of changes, a committee or commission appointed at intervals of twenty or twenty-five years (or even ten years) as in pre-Independence days, will not suffice. What we need is a permanent Administrative Reforms Council or Commission to oversee the whole programme of administrative reforms and to consider more fundamental questions like the ones indicated above which are beyond the powers of

Administrative Reforms Departments. This council should also supervise the implementation of the reforms suggested by the Administrative Reforms Organisation.

14. Such a permanent Administrative Reforms Council should be a small compact body consisting of :

- (i) The Minister of *State* in charge of General Administration;
- (ii) One MLA—from the Opposition;
- (iii) One Management Expert;
- (iv) The Addl. or Joint Secretary in charge of the Organisation which, as state above, should be under the Finance Ministry or Department.

15. The Management Expert who may perhaps be the only person outside the machinery of the State may be paid an allowance for attending the meetings of the Commission and if necessary a small honorarium. The MLA and the Managements Expert should have a term of not more than 5 years. The other two members *viz.* the Minister of State and the Secretary will normally be changed from time to time. This will ensure that the organisation does not become stale.

Role of Employees

16. Although a formal Administrative Reforms Organisation with a Council or Commission at the top is essential, every individual employee of Government has also an important role to play in improving administration and they have to be encouraged with prizes, awards or other incentives likely additional increments; but much more motivating would be non-monetary incentives like the Padmashri award given to Mr. Lakhina for the Ahmednagar Experiment. The British rulers had a remarkable way of motivating people with titles; but since titles have been abolished by the Constitution and since awards like Padmashri cannot be made too cheap, it is worthwhile experimenting with—

- (a) monetary rewards for minor reforms;
- (b) monetary rewards with medals for more important reforms. Since medals are given to Police and Army officers, why should they not be given to other civil servants?

Role of Consultants

17. Immediately after Independence in the fifties and the sixties many Governments engaged quite a few consultants from the private sector to suggest improvements in the working of Governments. At least so far as administrative offices were concerned, they were not of much help. The reason was that most of these consultants with Engineering or Accounts background looked at the problems of Government offices in a mechanistic way or from an accounts point of view as in the private sector. They would try to study forms used in Government offices or try to make studies of problems like the time spent by an officer in answering telephone calls or in attending meetings. These were often done with stop-watches as on the factory floor; but most of the problems and inefficiencies of Government arise from constraints imposed by laws and rules, inadequate delegations, unpredictability of funds and political interference. A Government Work study is, therefore, like a psycho-analytical examination in which the real problems of the department have to be ferreted out by talking to people and by study of several files.

18. In the sixties some attempt was made to develop Work Study and Management organisations in Government but as explained earlier, except in the Government of India, these organisations are in a shambles. It is time Governments made another attempt to develop their own organisations for Management studies. Till then, Government may have to take the help of private consultants in some high-tech areas like computers, project evaluation, and controls.

21

COMMITTEES

Government Offices are often required to deal with committees. There is supposed to be a science of "Committology" with several jokes about committees, such as (a) when Government departments wish to avoid taking a decision or action on any issue, they appoint a committee; (b) the best way to smother an issue is to appoint a committee; (c) if by chance we do receive the report of a committee quicker than expected, appoint another committee to examine the recommendations of the first committee..........

2. It cannot be denied that committees are often frustrating. Perhaps the best example of a committee which disappointed many people was the Administrative Reforms Commission which took nearly seven years to produce its report of more than 550 recommendations most of which ended up in pigeon-holes in the Government of India. However, as pointed out in chapter 20 on Administrative Reforms, committees have a useful role to play not only in government but also in all large organisations. The main advantages of a committee are —

(1) Where there is a controversial problem involving the interests of a large number of parties or organisations, it is necessary to secure the consensus of the majority of parties involved;

(2) In technical matters where it is necessary to consult persons of different disciplines, it is much better to constitute a committee rather than consult each expert or department separately;

(3) There are problems which cannot be tackled even by the highest officers in a department and in such cases a committee with a chairman and members of a sufficiently high status can carry more weight.

3. How can we make committees more effective? The present author who has worked as secretary of four Committees and Commissions of the Government of Maharashtra would recommend the following suggestions to be borne in mind:-

(1) Keep the size of the committee as small as possible. As far as possible do not include members who are known to be personally hostile to each other.

(2) In matters of day-to-day work (such as stores purchase) for which usually there are standing or permanent committees, the members should not be of too high a status as it is often difficult to secure the presence of such members frequently for meetings.

(3) Wherever possible and especially in the case of technical experts, if any member is unable to attend a meeting, he should be permitted to send a subordinate officer as his representative with proper briefing.

(4) The chairman of the committee should be a person with a sufficiently high status (depending upon the nature of the problem) with qualities of leadership and ability to control meetings. He should *preferably* be a person with good knowledge of the subject.

(5) The Secretary of a committee *must* be a person well-versed in the subject with a much wider knowledge of the subject than what an average Government officer gathers from the files.

(6) Before calling the first meeting, the secretary and the chairman should prepare a comprehensive note outlining the problem, the issues involved and tentative solutions. This prevents the committee from rambling from one subject to another like a rudderless ship. (If there are any technical problems the departments concerned should be consulted before preparing the note).

(7) At the end of every meeting fix the date for the next meeting. In the case of standing committees, there should, as far as possible, be a fixed day or date for meetings.

22

PUBLIC RELATIONS

While teaching "Management in Government" at some of the Institutes of Management in Bombay, I used to begin the course by giving the students (more than 90% of whom were from the private sector), a small exercise asking them to write down in three or four pages whatever they knew and felt about Government. Practically all of them (except about 5–10% who came from Government departments) used to write that all the Govt. offices and employees are inefficient, indifferent and corrupt.

2. Leaving aside for the present, the charge of corruption, one cannot deny the other allegations which apply in varying degrees to all Government departments. Government offices however, do not bother much about this poor image of theirs in the public mind; but with the press and the public now getting more and more active, they cannot hereafter ignore this problem.

3. The unfavourable impression about Government is formed on two planes :–

(i) on the public plane when the press or an active individual reports about some incident of gross mismanagement, waste or neglect by a Govt. department;

(ii) on the individual plane when an individual approaches Government about some problem and receives very unsatisfactory treatment from the office.

4. About public complaints, quite often they are based on some misunderstanding but Govt. offices rarely bother to reply to these complaints till their attention is drawn to these reports by some official

agency. Any rebuttal of the criticism is usually published after about two or three weeks when the people have practically forgotten the incident but not the impression created by it. Government offices – particularly senior officers should be very alert about such criticism in the public and see that rebuttals are issued within two or three days.

5. While these incidents on the public plane are often forgotten after some time, the unfavourable experiences of an individual, howsoever small, last much longer – sometimes for life.

6. An individual forms an unfavourable impression about Government–

(i) when he writes to the Govt. office about some question in which he is interested but does not get a reply for months even after reminding several times; and

(ii) when he visits a Govt. office but is either cold–shouldered or tossed like a shuttlecock from table to table without getting a satisfactory reply. This is basically due to the ignorance or inefficiency of the office which is due to two reasons – viz. – (a) the quality of the people working in the organisation, and (b) the systems in the organisation.

7. Regarding the people, there is no reason to suppose that Govt. employees who come from the same stock of people in the society, are in any way different from or inferior to the people in private or business organisations; but after entering Government they do develop some mental attitudes from the culture of that organisation – the most common of which are a rather low regard for efficiency and indifference or lack of sensitivity to the problems of the people. This is primarily due to what Mr. A.D. Gorwalla (an illustrious administrator of yore) called the "darbari" soil of this country where we regard a member of the public as a ryot begging for some favour or justice from "ma–baap Sarkar", forgetting that the Constitution has given him some fundamental rights.

8. It is difficult to eradicate this age old traditional attitude in a very short period. Courses in public relations or a few lectures given to Government officers may not make much impact. Many offices have Public Relations Officers or Reception Officers but quite often these are rejects from the department who are considered unfit for the line work of the department. In many offices these PROs are assigned the duty of looking after VIPs like Ministers. It is time Governments (Union as well

as States) create cadres of good PROs for offices with large public contacts, such as the Income Tax Department, the Customs Department or the Collectors' Offices. These need not be brilliant first class graduates from the universities or chiffon-clad dolls sitting at elegant reception desks but people who have worked in some non-government organisations (NGOs) with some experience of working in rural areas.

9. The other important reason for the apparent indifference or inefficiency of Government is to be found in the system. As explained in Chapter 2, there are some basic differences between public administration and business administration particularly the severe accountability of public administration to the legislature, the judiciary, the press and the people, which imposes some serious limitations on the speed and efficiency of the Government system; but as explained in Chapter 2, many of these limitations are overdone by the timidity, the stupidity and sometimes even the cupidity of some government servants. In Chapters 10–14, we have indicated how some of these systems can be improved by changing procedures, by delegations and by giving prompt replies. To repeat some of the suggestion made in those chapters–

- (i) Issue acknowledgement cards for all first letters and by issuing *ad interim* replies whenever he reminds;
- (ii) In the case of routine applications for licences, permits etc. scrutinise the application at the receiving counters and do not accept it unless it is complete in all respects; if it is incomplete explain to the applicant the deficiencies in his application. For this purpose the person at the receiving counter should be an experienced one, and not a raw recruit from the Employment Exchange.
- (iii) If the application is complete, give the applicant a suitable date when he can call again for a reply;
- (iv) Prepare small pamphlets explaining in respect of most matters for which the people approach the office, the Government policies, programmes and procedures (see the Ahmednagar Experiment in Appendix A).

10. The lack of discipline in most Government offices make a very poor first impression on visitors. Government and semi-government offices allow the employees a grace-period of ten to fifteen minutes in attending the office in the morning. This is meant for contingencies like

traffic blocks or trains running late; but the employees treat it as if the office time is 10.10 a.m. instead of 10.00 a.m. What is still worse, many of the Personnel Officers (called Establishment Officers in Government) who are supposed to keep a watch on the attendance of employees, themselves never come in time.

11. After coming to the office (usually ten to fifteen minutes late) the employees make a bee-line for the canteen so that a visitor who arrives at the office at the opening hour, has to wait for twenty to thirty minutes to meet the concerned employee. You find that even bank employees are often not at their counters on time.

(It may not be out of place to narrate an interesting experience of the present author. He was working on a report with the assistance of another junior officer. The office time then was 10.00 a.m. While the author usually came to the office about ten to fifteen minutes before time, his colleague always used to come by about 10.20 a.m.; so the work could not be started before 10.30 a.m.

The author asked his colleague if he could not come a bit earlier by taking an earlier train. He was amused to hear from his colleague that the earlier train was *too* early; it would bring him to office by 9.55 a.m. So the gentleman did not mind coming late by twenty minutes but was a "conscientious objector" to coming five minutes before time).

12. It is worthwhile trying the following measures–

(1) Abolish the practice of grace time if necessary by changing the office time. If the office time is 10.00 a.m. change it to 10.15 a.m., if necessary, but insist on everybody being in his seat by 10.15 a.m.

(2) Except during the lunch hour, office canteens should be closed during working hours.

(3) Tea may be served to employees at the table during working hours.

(4) There should be a special cadre of Establishment Officers selected for their reputation for discipline.

13. It is relevant to mention here that one public sector undertaking in Maharashtra with a strict disciplinarian as a Managing Director had prescribed a muster even for officers.

14. Another feature of Government offices which creates a poor image of Government is the system of casual leave. This is again a special feature of Government offices in India which has now spread even to the

private sector. (There is no system of casual leave in most of the developed countries in the West).

15. The public sector undertaking in Maharashtra referred to earlier in para 13, had managed to reduce (if not eliminate) the scourge of casual leave by the following measures–

(i) The quota of casual leave was fixed at 10 days in a year (as against 15 days in Government);

(ii) Encashment of unenjoyed casual leave was allowed at 1.5 times the normal salary rate so that many employees earned nearly half a month's salary like a bonus every year. (The system of bonus had not yet been extended to Government offices);

(iii) The House Keeping Section which looked after the maintenance of office premises, cars, furniture etc. was asked to make arrangements for sundry jobs of employees like payment of bills, insurance premia, renewal of licences, permits etc.

The result was that the incidence of casual leave in the undertaking was just about 3 days per employee per annum. Is it impossible to introduce this system in Government offices?

APPENDIX -A

THE AHMEDNAGAR EXPERIMENT

Dr. S.S. Gadkari

(Article published in "Ambit" the Journal of the Bombay Management Association in 1983)

Referring to some of our development projects like steel plants and hydel projects, Pandit Nehru once said that these are our new temples and places of pilgrimages. One wonders how Pandit Nehru (who did not have a very high opinion about administration and administrators) would have reacted if he were to be told that a Collector's office in a not too well-known district in Maharashtra had become a place of pilgrimage not only for administrators from all over India but academicians from Management Institutes, journalists, eminent litterateurs and even film producers. The name of Mr. Anil Kumar Lakhina the young Collector of Ahmednagar, has broken all the veils or shrouds of anonymity which are supposed to shield all Government servants from public gaze and still more from public admiration. He has received tributes from all quarters. The Governor of Maharashtra for example, asked for some old records and when these were produced in a few minutes, he is reported to have remarked that this was like magic. Mr. P.L. Deshpande one of the most eminent Marathi writers said "It is an unusual experience to feel so cheerful on entering a Government office".

2. Study teams from other States and Management institutions have also visited the Collectorate and even newspapers have published articles praising the work of the Collector. The Government of Maharashtra sent a study team of senior Secretaries which studied what has now come to be known as the "Ahmednagar Experiment" and recommended its extention to six other districts which were given special grants of Rs. 1 lakh each for the purpose. (Mr. Lakhina did not require any special grant for effecting his improvements).

3. For the benefit of administrators and Management scientists it is necessary to rise above all this din and glare of publicity of popular reaction and try to understand what exactly the young Collector has done, to understand the "experiment" and evaluate it, repeat it wherever possible and even improve upon it. As the Chief Secretary of the Maharashtra Government said, "it is necessary to depersonalise the reforms and institutionalise them".

4. For the past 150 years the Collector has been the lynchpin of administration and has often rightly been called not only the eyes and ears of Government but even its hands and feet. In pre-Independence days his primary functions were collection of land revenue and maintenance of law and order. Independence and even the establishment of Panchayati Raj institutions have not diminished the importance of the Collector who has been and is, being saddled with more and more functions like the distribution of scarce commodities, planning and development, not to mention the intolerable burden of attending to V.I.Ps. No attention has been paid to the organisation of collectors' offices to meet their evergrowing functions and responsibilities. The Collectors' offices continue in the same old buildings spread over large compounds with people roaming about or clustered in groups like stray cattle. The old dilapidated buildings have usually had not even a lime-wash for years; or if it has, it is probably due to an error as Mr. Lakhina has aptly put it. The furniture consists of chairs and tables of odd sizes strewn about in every room without any order or pattern. In such a dismal atmosphere the old fashioned clerk (most of whom have studied only upto S.S.C.) is usually surrounded by half a dozen visitors. His papers are spread over the table or stacked inside cupboards. Cases are often not touched till the party approaches him; and his first reply on any such approach is that he has not received the case. In such a situation the intercession of a middleman or a V.I.P. is considered essential to get anything done.

5. This is the picture in practically all the Collectorates or rather in all the offices in the mofussil. Committees and Commissions go into the reorganisation of the offices but their reports usually gather dust in the Secretariat for want of funds but more for lack of sufficient interest or drive in the Secretariat or the local Collectors who usually do not remain in one district for more than a year and a half. It is against this background that we should view the work of Mr. Lakhina. Within a space of a year or a year and a half he has so transformed the Collector's Office that (as stated in the opening paragraph) it has become a place of pilgrimage for people from all corners of the country and from all walks of life.

6. Mr. Lakhina has graciously acknowledged that he was not the

first to try this experiment. Earlier, another Collector Mr. V.P. Raja had attempted to improve the working conditions and the system of contact with the public in the Satara District. Mr. Lakhina sent teams of officers to study the Satara experiment and it was after this study that the plan for this epoch making experiment was drawn.

Broadly this plan was based on four basic pillars:

(1) Improved working environment;
(2) Regulation of staff—public contact;
(3) Improved records management;
(4) Demystification of Government work.

Improving Work Environment and Regulation of Staff-Public Contact

7. The Ahmednagar Collectorate is spread over four or five detached 150 year old buildings. The woodwork, the walls, the ceiling had not been painted for years. The once white-washed walls were covered with pictures of gods, goddesses and cine-stars, publicity posters and scribbled with telephone numbers and addresses. The furniture pieces were in odd sizes and arranged without any order, each clerk aligning his table according to his preference for position. Ahmednagar being a comparatively dry district, the furniture and papers were usually covered with plenty of dust. The Collector, therefore, took the following steps:

(i) painting the walls, doors, windows, ceiling in some pleasing shades;
(ii) black-topping all the open areas in the compound to reduce dust nuisance;
(iii) removing all the junk in the compound of the Collector's office and making it clean and tidy;
(iv) preparing a proper lay-out for the office with the help of local architects (who gladly agreed to do all this work free);
(v) standardising the size of furniture and arranging it systematically, each clerk being provided with a standard sized table and a rack;
(vi) improvement of toilets and water supply facilities and provision of good lunch-rooms for the staff; and
(vii) covering the floor with simple jute carpets and placing a few plants in each room.

8. All this was done without any extra grant from Government. It is worth noting that Mr. Lakhina did not buy any new furniture but only reallocated the existing furniture so that the tables and chairs in each room were more or less of uniform size.

9. A feature of the new layout was the reduction of access for members of the public to the office. They could only see officers. Earlier, the office looked more like a village market with members of the public swarming all over the place. Officers' cabins which were placed next to their office staff were provided with transparent glass partitions improving supervision over the staff.

10. A pleasant environment is the minimum that every office should have. It is something taken for granted in a private sector office but is rather difficult to come by in Government offices. This is partly due to the poor provision for maintenance but more due to the lack of consciousness about a pleasant environment on the part of most Government officers and Mr. Lakhina deserves congratulations for creating this consciousness among his staff. The infection is also now spreading to other Government offices in the district. Even the Maharashtra Government Secretariat has weeded out a large proportion of old records and cleared practically all the corridors of the Secretariat of cupboards. If the Ahmednagar Experiment leads to a change in the attitude of Government offices towards office environment, it can indeed be called a revolutionary change.

Improved Records Management

11. More important than the environmental improvement was the improvement in the maintenance of records. Non availability of records is a common excuse in Government offices. This is all the more regrettable because the "Memory" function of office is far more important in Government than in the private sector. This non-availability of records is usually due to failure to follow very good systems laid down for the Revenue Department during pre-Independence days. The Collector of Ahmednagar only ensured the implementation of these systems under which the papers with each clerk are kept in six bundles as follows:

(i) Current papers pending disposal;
(ii) Await cases (*i.e.* those kept pending for want of some report or information or decision on some case);
(iii) Periodical Reports;
(iv) Standing order files;
(v) Papers to be sent to the Record Office;

(vi) Papers to be destroyed at the end of the year.

Each clerk was provided with an open rack and closed almirahs were removed except for keeping confidential documents.

12. The record room which earlier looked more like an unkempt paper godown, had not been touched for twenty to thirty years. It was improved beyond recognition. The unwanted papers were weeded out and the remaining papers were neatly tied in bundles showing the subject and the date of the record. An index-card system at the entrance to the Record Room further facilitated accessibility to record. Ten truckloads of weeded out papers fetched nearly Rs. 26,000 for the Government Treasury.

Demystification of Government-work

13. To the common man a Government office is "an enigma wrapped in mystery". He is unaware of the procedures in a Government office or the requirements of the laws and regulations. He sends in a simple application for a licence or a permit. For weeks and months he doesn't know what is happening to his application. Ultimately it comes back to him with a rejection letter or a demand for some more particulars in official gibberish. In a large number of cases the letter vanishes in the labyrinth of the office. In such a situation touts have a field day and most people believe that you can never get anything done at a government office without the help of a tout or a V.I.P.

14. The Collector of Ahmednagar, therefore, launched a system of demystification of Government work. Two important measures were introduced in this respect—

(i) Education of the public by the preparation of simple pamphlets explaining the procedure to be followed, the documents to be submitted in respect of the various types of cases; and

(ii) In respect of purely routine and repetitive types of work like renewal of licences etc., a counter was established where the application was scrutinised before being accepted. If the application was in order the applicant was given a token and asked to come on a specified day—when the licence or permit would be ready. If the application was incomplete, it was not accepted but the applicant was told at the counter what was lacking.

An Assessment of the Experiment

15. The efficiency and effectiveness of an office and particularly a Government office depends upon the following factors:

(i) The quality of the staff working in the office;
(ii) The tools available to the staff (of which records form an important element in the case of Government offices);
(iii) The methods and procedures of work which often form a serious constraint on efficiency in the case of Government offices;
(iv) The office environment; and
(v) Relationship with the clients.

16. The Ahmednagar Experiment tackled successfully two of these factors *viz.* (ii) the tools and (iv) the environment. It has also made a serious attempt to improve (v) relationship with the clients—particularly in the matter of issue of licences and permits—by its process of demystification and the system of issuing licences etc. across the counter in many cases.

17. As for the quality of the staff, the Collector like most Government officers, has very little control over the hiring and firing of his staff and has to accept whatever staff is in position; and due to the poor standards of remuneration and other factors like reservation for Backward Classes, the quality of staff in Government offices is usually not upto the mark. But it must be said to the credit of the Collector that he was able to motivate this staff remarkably and they all worked as a team for more than a year to put the office records in order and to implement the other measures. During his brief stay at Ahmednagar the writer took the opportunity to talk to some of the staff without the intervention of any of their officers and he found them proud of their achievements. This motivation was further improved by training programmes started by the Collector. These measures to some extent made up for the initial poor quality of the staff.

18. There was, however, very little attempt to tackle the methods and procedures of work probably because in the case of Revenue Offices these are to a large extent decided by rules and regulations framed by Government. The Collector himself in a monograph on the Experiment has suggested a study of the methods and procedures by the Secretariat.

19. This, I feel, was not the right approach for two reasons:

(i) Even though the broad procedures are laid down by the rules, regulations and manuals made by Government, there are always local variations in each office; and

(ii) Proposals for modification should come from the local officers who are in a better position to know where the shoe pinches. In the sixties the State Government established work study units. This writer's experience as a Work Study officer was that a large proportion of the suggestions for improvement emerged from discussion with the staff and not by the study of rules and manuals.

20. This study of procedures and methods is often more fruitful than other mechanical improvements such as issuing licences or permits across counters in six hours because such studies often indicate that the licence or permit can be altogether dispensed with thereby relieving both the office as well as the client of the need to go through the whole routine, however, simplified. In particular delegation of powers to lower officers (which may require amendment of rules and regulations) can eliminate a large amount of work in an office.

APPENDIX–B

SOME ILLUSTRATIVE INDEXING SYSTEMS

I. Government of India—"Conventional" system

This is based entirely on numbers as can be seen from the following example:

(1) File No. 3/1/74 Public I
(2) File No. 3/2/74 Public I

In the above numbers—

3 represent a subject.

1 and 2 - represent the serial No. of the file under the standard head.

74 — Indicates the year in which the file was opened.

Public I — Indicates the Section to which the file pertains.

In this system based entirely on numbers, the file No. does not in any way indicate even the broad subject.

II. Government of India—Functional Indexing System

Example (1) File No. A 32013/6/72- Adm. IA

In this—

A — stands for the functional group "*Administration*"

32 — stands for the primary head "Appointment"

0 — is a separator.

13 — stands for the secondary head — Class II Posts.

6 — indicates that this is the 6th file under the head opened during the year

72 — stands for the year 1972.

Adm IA — stands for the number of the Section.

Example (2)— File No. IV - 13024/5/71- LRI

In this —

IV	—	represents the functional group Labour Relations
13	—	stands for the primary head "strikes"
0	—	is the separator
24	—	stands for the secondary head coal mines
5	—	indicates that it is the 5th file under the head opened during the year.
71	—	stands for the year of opening the file
LRI	—	represents the section concerned.

There are, to my mind, two defects in the system—

(i) The functional groups indicated by simple letters, (A, B, C, D) or Roman No. IV do not at first sight give any idea of the subject unless one refers to the indexing system; and

(ii) The use of 0 for the separation of the primary and secondary heads is likely to cause confusion. Instead, separation by an oblique (/) or horizontal (-) stroke would be better.

III. Tri-letter Indexing System in the Maharashtra Secretariat

The system of giving index numbers to files in the Maharashtra Secretariat is fairly simple and practical. The file number has 6 parts as show in the examples below:

	(1)	(2) (3)	(4)	(5)	(6)
(1)	MUN -	25-92 /	7581 /	CR - 456/	18
(2)	WSS -	31-93 /	14382 /	CR - 565 /	15
(3)	TPL -	42-87 /	44381 /	CR - 379 /	23

Here —

(1) the three letters MUN, WSS, TPL indicate the broad subject such as—

MUN - for municipalities

WSS - for Water Supply and Sewerage

TPL - for Town Planning.

(2) The numbers 25, 31, 42 in the next column indicate the detailed subject such as—

25 - for Municipal Taxation

31 - for Water Supply for Nagpur

42 - for Town Planning Schemes for Aurangabad district.

(3) The next two figures 92, 93, 87 indicate the year in which the file was started.

(4) the next numbers 7581, 14382, 44381 show the Inward Register number given to the first communication on the file. (The inward numbers of all the communications on the file are entered on the docket sheet of the file).

(5) The next numbers CR - 456, CR - 565, CR - 379 indicate the number of the case in the Case Register. Every file or paper does not become a case. Simple papers such as a letter asking for a copy of some orders, or a copy of a letter sent for information to the Deptt. are not entered in the Case Register.

(6) The last number (18, 15, 13) indicates the number of the Section dealing with the case.

The great merit of the system is that the tri-letters immediately indicate the broad subject like Municipalities or Town Planning or Water Supply and Sewerage.

IV. System in the Haryana Secretariat

A file No. has 6 parts as shown below :

		(1)	(2)	(3)	(4)	(5)
(i)	File No.	1 /	1/	92/	Est -	I / 7E
(ii)	File No.	1 /	6 /	84 /	Est -	I/7E
(iii)	File No.	2 /	1 /	93 /	Est -	I /1E
(iv)	File No.	2 /	2 /	92 /	Est -	I / 1E

(1) The *first* number indicates the *main head* of the subject such as—
1 – for "Creation and classification of posts"
2 – for "Recruitment"

(2) The *second* number indicates the detailed subject such as -
1—for "Continuation of temporary posts in the Haryana Civil Service"
6 - for "Continuation of temporary posts in the Economic Ser vices"
1 - for "Appointment of Assistant Planning Officer"
2 - for "Appointment of District Attorney"

(3) The *third* figure indicates the year in which the file was started.

(4) The *fourth* number "Est - I" indicates the Section to which the file pertain.

(5) The *last* number and letter - (7E or 1E) shows the designation (*i.e.* the table) of the person in the section who deals with the subject.

This is also a purely numerical system where the number of the file does not give any indication of the subject.

The last number indicating the table number to which the paper pertains is, however, a useful indicator.

V. Orissa Secretariat System

The file number has 5 parts as in the following example :—

		(1)	(2)	(3)	(4)
(1)	File No. —	AIS —	— I	—1	—92-93
(2)	File No. —	Trg —	I/(F)	—2	—84-85

Here:—

(1) The tri-letters indicate the broad subject such as —

AIS — for All India Services

Trg — for Training

(2) The Second figures I/II or the letters I/F, indicate the detailed subject such as—

I — for Cadre questions

II — for Appointments

III — for Deputation, Transfer, Posting ....etc.

(I) — for training within the country

(F) — for foreign training.

(3) The next part (1/2) indicates the number assigned to each individual file in the files Register maintained by the Assistant.

(4) The last part (92-93) or (84-85) indicates the year in which the file was opened.

The tri-letters indicate the subject; but there is no indication in this system of the Section to which it pertains. This is indicated on the file cover. This however, is not enough because when a letter is received in the Department, the Receiving Clerk may not be able to guess the Section unless he is familiar with the subjects in each section.

Appendix - B

KERALA

The file number like the one shown below, has 5 parts as explained below:

I	II	III	IV	V
No. 999/	Est-	D/1	93 /	Agri

Here

Part I (999) — shows the inward register number with which the file was started.

Part II (Est) — shows the section where it is dealt with

Part III (D 1) — shows the table or desk of the Establishment section where it is dealt with

Part IV (93) — shows the year in which the file was started

Part V (Agri) — shows the name of the department where the file is dealt with.

There is nothing in the number to indicate the detailed subject except that it is something connected with Establishment (or Personnel) matters. It can be a file about promotions, transfers, leave, provident fund advance, ...

The last part indicating the name of Department seems to be superfluous since the name of the department is usually indicated in the printed letter-head or typed at the top of the letter.

Note : Information about the system in the Central Secretariat has been taken from a publication of the Central Secretaiat Training Institute while information about other State Governments was obtained by correspondence with the respective Secretariats. There may be some mistakes but these examples are given only for illustration.

INDEX

I

J

L

M

N

O

P